MALVERN WOMEN OF NOTE

MALVERN
WOMEN *of* NOTE

PAMELA HURLE

Malvern Women of Note
Pamela Hurle

Published by Aspect Design 2012
Malvern, Worcestershire, United Kingdom.

Designed, printed and bound by Aspect Design
89 Newtown Road, Malvern, Worcs. WR14 1PD
United Kingdom
Tel: 01684 561567
E-mail: books@aspect-design.net
Website: www.aspect-design.net

ISBN 978-1-908832-18-4

CONTENTS

LIST OF ILLUSTRATIONS

INTRODUCTION

This short book has its origins in a talk I was asked to give in 2001 to Malvern Museum Association to mark the centenary of the death of Queen Victoria in 1901. Entitled *Some Victorian Ladies of Malvern*, it was largely concerned with the aristocratic ladies of the area but recognised the importance of those lower in the rigid social scale of earlier times.

In the last eleven years, having looked intermittently at other women who played a part in Malvern's history, I was very pleased when Peter Smith, who in 1989 founded the Autumn in Malvern Festival, invited me to give a talk in 2012 on Malvern women of note.

The significance of these women, often reaching places far distant from Malvern, is, however, such that I feel that their contribution should be noted in a form more permanent than an hour's lecture. If this book brings out of the shadows some remarkable women whose influence has been forgotten it will have done what was needed.

ACKNOWLEDGEMENTS

For granting me permission to use some of the illustrations in this book I wish to thank Freda Ballard, Humphrey Bartleet for his family pictures of Lady Foley, Malvern St James archivist Elisabeth Rambridge, Malvern Library staff and Peter Smith, who also suggested the title and made informed and helpful comment on my text. I am delighted that Aspect Design, loyal supporters of the Autumn in Malvern Festival and a family business with which it has always been a pleasure to work, have printed and published it.

Most of all I thank my husband who has constantly supported me through so many years, and dedicate this book to him, slightly belatedly, to mark our golden wedding anniversary.

Pamela Hurle
Autumn 2012

ARISTOCRATIC LADIES OF MALVERN

Since our society has for generations been dominated by class it is almost inevitable that the aristocracy first come to mind in considering those women who have influenced affairs in Malvern. Some might say that the woman who most influenced the development of Malvern was Queen Victoria, since the town is often called a Victorian town. Realistically, however, Victoria came here only for a few weeks in 1830, when she was a child accompanied by her dominant mother, the Duchess of Kent. They stayed at Holly Mount, a large house that stood above the Worcester Road, behind Brays, the department store founded in the nineteenth century and still very popular. The adult Victoria never came to Malvern, though the town loyally named roads and a public park after her and members of her family, as well as celebrating her jubilees with bonfires and stained glass windows in Great Malvern Priory.

The first chapter of this book looks at a few remarkable ladies who exercised a more direct benign despotism in and around Malvern. Perhaps, in several cases, one might wonder if their influence was so strong not simply because of their class but also because they worked without the restraining hand of a husband at a time when women – and married women especially – looked to the men in their families for direction and for financial support. Even Queen Victoria did the former, if not the latter.

Malvern always remembered Princess Victoria's childhood visit, and loyally commemorated her Golden Jubilee in fitting style with a stained glass window in the north aisle of Great Malvern Priory Church. Key events in her life are pictured in three lower lights. The first shows her as an eighteen year old girl on the summer morning in 1837 when she was told of the death of her Uncle William, meaning that she was now monarch; the second portrays her coronation and the third the thanksgiving service for her long and successful reign. The last is a remarkable portrayal in an English church of the queen's grand-son Wilhelm, later to be Germany's Kaiser, standing behind her in the window glass. After the First War World many shocked and bereaved Britons joined the shout of 'Hang the Kaiser', whom they understandably but unfairly blamed for causing a war with such a horrendous death toll.

Mary, Countess Harcourt (1749–1833)

John Chambers dedicated his 1817 *History of Malvern* to 'Mary, Countess Harcourt whose taste and benevolence has embellished and benefited Malvern.' In the manner of his time he unctuously thanked her for encouraging him to write his history and summed up her life. The daughter of the Revd William Danby of Yorkshire, she was widowed in her mid-twenties and, still in her twenties, in 1778 married the third Earl Harcourt. He had distinguished himself by capturing the commander of the American Army, General Lee, in the war for American independence.

Earl Harcourt's biographer in the *Dictionary of National Biography* was rather less flattering about the Countess than Chambers chose to be, quoting that she was 'a woman of warm temper and small reserve,' with a reputation for meddling and, sometimes, spite.[1] Nevertheless, she and her husband were generous and, like many of their class, took their social obligations as seriously as their rights.

---

1. R. N. W. Thomas, *Oxford Dictionary of National Biography*, entry on William Harcourt.

They both repeatedly gave to good causes such as the repair of Great Malvern Priory Church and its windows and the establishment of a Sunday School at Little Malvern. Harcourt Road is a reminder of their presence and generosity.

Her main achievement, however, was paying for the construction of paths on the hills after she came with her husband to Malvern in the early nineteenth century. Although this was some thirty years before the water-cure attracted visitors to Malvern, she felt that basic facilities were lacking. In 1817 John Chambers wrote:

Holly Mount where the young Princess Victoria stayed. Later, in the 1860s, it briefly housed the staff and girls of the school which became known as Lawnside.
Courtesy Malvern St James.

When Lady Harcourt first visited Malvern, there was but one small path to the top of the hills, and this led to the least interesting part of them ... It has ever been her ladyship's delight ... to form several walks in the most picturesque parts of the Malvern Hills, particularly round the beautiful camp hill, for a distance of about five miles ....[2]

He claimed she would have extended the paths 'from the wells to Great Malvern' but was prevented from doing so by 'the different

2. John Chambers, *A General History of Malvern*, p.192.

proprietors of the hill, who, with the exception of Mr Hornyold, impeded her progress.' Such controversy, about seventy years before the foundation of the Malvern Hills Conservators in 1884, was a foretaste of the high feelings which were aroused when people felt that their rights, as landowners and as farmers grazing their animals on the common, were in any way threatened. Chambers' comment shows that, even in the very early nineteenth century, locals with traditional rights were already resisting challenges from those who saw the Malvern Hills as a recreation area. Lady Harcourt clearly backed off – two generations later a group of men had the confidence and power to seek a compromise between the two, establishing the Malvern Hills Conservators to implement it.

Lady Harcourt's well-intentioned efforts were further indicated by her paying for two shelters: Harcourt Tower on Pinnacle Hill and Harcourt Alcove on the Worcestershire Beacon. The iron roof on the Alcove, however, was a fatal design fault: it was struck by lightning in 1826, killing four young walkers who had taken refuge in it during a thunderstorm. Three of them were sisters whose two brothers were seriously injured. This terrible loss and shock for their family – the Hills who farmed in Dymock – was shared by the family of the fourth young fatality, Helen Woodyatt of Hereford.[3]

Chambers noted that Lady Harcourt also provided seats and left £100, the interest on which was to be spent on the repair of the seats. In this, too, she was well ahead of her times.

Apphia, Lady Lyttelton (1743–1840)

The name of Apphia, Lady Lyttelton, is familiar because of the Malvern buildings named after her – the Lyttelton School and the Lyttelton buildings where Malvern's thriving Museum started its life in the late 1970s.

Born in the Cotswolds in 1743, she was the second daughter of Broome Witts of Chipping Norton. In 1769 she went to India to marry her cousin – a long and uncomfortable journey a hundred years before the building of the Suez Canal – and by the time she

---

3. T. C. Turberville, *Worcestershire in the Nineteenth Century*, p.262.

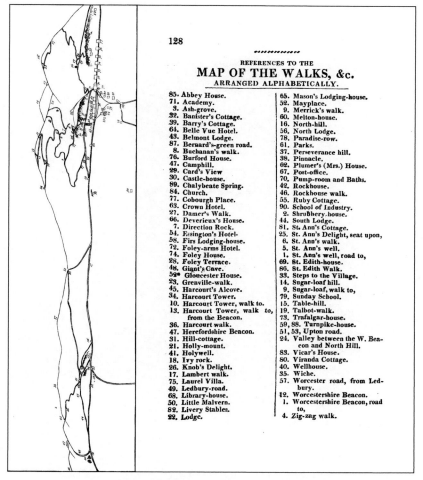

128

●●●●●●●●●●

REFERENCES TO THE

MAP OF THE WALKS, &c.
ARRANGED ALPHABETICALLY.

85. Abbey House.
71. Academy.
3. Ash-grove.
32. Banister's Cottage.
39. Barry's Cottage.
64. Belle Vue Hotel.
43. Belmont Lodge.
87. Bernard's-green road.
8. Buchanan's walk.
76. Burford House.
47. Camphill.
29. Card's View
30. Castle-house.
89. Chalybeate Spring.
84. Church.
77. Cobourgh Place.
63. Crown Hotel.
27. Damer's Walk.
66. Devereux's House.
7. Direction Rock.
54. Essington's Hotel.
58. Firs Lodging-house.
72. Foley-arms Hotel.
74. Foley House.
28. Foley Terrace.
48. Giant's Cave.
52* Gloucester House.
23. Grenville-walk.
45. Harcourt's Alcove.
34. Harcourt Tower.
10. Harcourt Tower, walk to.
13. Harcourt Tower, walk to, from the Beacon.
36. Harcourt walk.
47. Herefordshire Beacon.
31. Hill-cottage.
21. Holly-mount.
41. Holywell.
18. Ivy rock.
26. Knob's Delight.
17. Lambert walk.
75. Laurel Villa.
49. Ledbury-road.
68. Library-house.
50. Little Malvern.
82. Livery Stables.
22. Lodge.

65. Mason's Lodging-house.
52. Mayplace.
9. Merrick's walk.
60. Melton-house.
16. North-hill.
56. North Lodge.
78. Paradise-row.
61. Parks.
37. Perseverance hill.
38. Pinnacle.
62. Plumer's (Mrs.) House.
67. Post-office.
70. Pump-room and Baths.
42. Rockhouse.
46. Rockhouse walk.
55. Ruby Cottage.
90. School of Industry.
2. Shrubbery-house.
44. South Lodge.
81. St. Ann's Cottage.
25. St. Ann's Delight, seat upon,
6. St. Ann's walk.
5. St. Ann's well.
1. St. Ann's well, road to,
69. St. Edith-house.
86. St. Edith Walk.
33. Steps to the Village.
14. Sugar-loaf hill.
9. Sugar-loaf, walk to,
79. Sunday School.
15. Table-hill.
19. Talbot-walk.
73. Trafalgar-house.
59, 88. Turnpike-house.
51, 53, Upton road.
24. Valley between the W. Beacon and North Hill.
83. Vicar's House.
80. Viranda Cottage.
40. Wellhouse.
35. Wiche.
57. Worcester road, from Ledbury.
12. Worcestershire Beacon.
1. Worcestershire Beacon, road to,
4. Zig-zag walk.

Diagram of hill paths with key from the early nineteenth century, as shown in Mary Southall's *Description of Malvern*.

arrived he had died. At first planning to return home, she in fact met and married the wealthy Governor of Calcutta, Colonel Joseph Peach. He, too, died a few months after the wedding so she returned, a rich widow, to England and lived at the Leasowes, near Hagley, before marrying Thomas, the 'wicked' Lord Lyttelton in 1772. They were legally separated less than two years after the marriage. This

Lady Lyttelton.

fatally unhappy union was one where the sympathies of Thomas
Lyttelton's father lay with his daughter-in-law rather than his son.
On the face of it, this may seem surprising but the facts – his selfish
and dissolute behaviour contrasted with her modesty, common sense
and kindness – explain how this most unsatisfactory husband lost his
father's support. Born in 1744, educated at Eton and Christchurch
and known for his wit and oratory, Thomas Lyttelton was for a few
months the MP for Bewdley but lost his seat in January 1769. He
succeeded his father, the 'good' Lord Lyttelton, in 1773 but died
in 1779, aged thirty-four, leaving the wife with whom he had lived
so briefly a title, an annuity and no apparent desire for any further
attempts at marriage.

Lady Lyttelton came to Malvern about 1800 and died in 1840 a few days before her ninety-seventh birthday. In 1817 John Chambers referred to her in the sycophantic language of the class-conscious nineteenth century as 'one who has for many years exerted herself, and continues to watch over the morals of the lower orders of society around Malvern.'[4]

Her concern was revealed in her foundation of the Lyttelton School in the corner of the churchyard at Great Malvern Priory Church. This Sunday School was rebuilt in 1887, eventually became a boys' school, which closed in the 1940s and is now the heart of the Lyttelton Well complex:

> When her ladyship married Colonel Peach, he presented her with a valuable set of filagree dressing-plate. She determined ... to dedicate its value to some charitable purpose. She first intended to endow some houses for widows, but finding the state of children about Malvern was miserable, from a total want of religious instruction, she resolved to honour the memory of the donor by laudably applying his gift to the erection of a Sunday School.[5]

According to Grindrod, writing a Malvern guide book much later in the nineteenth century, Lady Lyttelton, who lived at Poolbrook in a house known as Peckham Grove, came to Malvern village and slept on Saturday evenings in a room adjoining the Sunday School so that she could help on the Sabbath.[6]

Lady Lyttelton was also a key contributor to a school of Industry at Poolbrook, described in some detail by John Chambers and by Mary Southall:

> An unadorned building was erected near Peckham Grove, her Ladyship's cottage, in which there is a room, 35 feet by 14,

---

4. John Chambers, *A General History of Malvern*, p.267.
5. Ibid.
6. Charles Grindrod, *Malvern Guide*, p.102.

suitable for the work carried on by children, who are taught to card and spin wool, flax and hemp, knitting and every kind of common needlework; such as making and mending coarse garments, jackets and linen for the use of their parents and themselves. In this manner they may learn to produce their own garments of a cheap and substantial kind, suitable to their condition in life, as in former ages. In order to preserve to society a useful hardy peasantry it is intended to encourage field-work; and that this employment may not be the means, as heretofore, of corrupting the morals of young persons, one

A modern picture of the Lyttelton building founded as a Sunday School.

of the matrons of the school always attends and works with them. Reading is regularly promoted; religious duties instilled and industry is encouraged by an exact account being kept of their respective earnings.[7]

When Lady Lyttelton died in 1840 her funeral was a major event in the village of Malvern. But the village was about to become a fashionable

7.   Mary Southall, *A Description of Malvern*, p.69.

At her Stoke Edith home Lady Emily Foley, lady of the manor of Malvern, is flanked by the Duke and Duchess of Teck when they visited Malvern for the duchess officially to open the new British Camp reservoir and waterworks in 1895. Second from left is their daughter, the future Queen Mary. On her right is Miss Winifred Herbert and on her left is the Very Revd George Herbert, Dean of Hereford with Miss Mary Herbert on his left.
Courtesy Humphrey Bartleet.

spa town ruled by an extraordinary widowed aristocratic lady of the manor whose influence was even greater than that of Lady Lyttelton.

Lady Emily Foley (1805–1900)
Lady Emily Foley, born on 23 June 1805, more than sixty years after Apphia Witts, was the daughter of the third Duke of Montrose, whose family name was Graham. At the age of twenty-seven Lady Emily Graham married the Honourable Edward Foley, nearly fourteen years her senior. The marriage produced no children and he died in 1846, leaving the extensive Foley property in trust and in her capable hands until her own death over fifty years later. The property included extensive estates in Staffordshire, Herefordshire and Worcestershire. Lady Emily found herself lady of the manor of Wednesbury as well as of Great Malvern, the Foley family having bought the latter in 1741.

The memorial in Stoke Edith church to Edward Thomas Foley and to his widow, Lady Emily.

Through her land steward she ruled Malvern from the Foley family's late seventeenth-century mansion at Stoke Edith, some few miles over the border into Herefordshire, but she came to stay in Malvern each summer to keep a careful eye on manorial affairs. Catherine Severn Burrow describes what an event was created by her arrival, carried along the Wells Road in her brightly painted yellow landau with its coachman, footman and postillion in striking livery of white breeches and stockings, strawberry coloured coats, black top hats and considerable gold lace. Welcomed at the outskirts of Malvern by a band, and to the town by the ringing of the Priory bells, she was greeted at the Foley Arms Hotel, where she stayed, by the vicar, churchwardens and chairman of the Town Commissioners.[8] They would be subjected to:

> … searching questions to which precise answers were required … During her stay she would tour the whole of her Malvern estate, starting with her agent and foreman at 9 o'clock, and lunching on sandwiches at some farm house with her exhausted attendants at 2 p.m.[9]

She was getting into her stride as matriarch of Malvern at exactly the time in the 1840s that the water-cure, pioneered here by Dr Wilson and Dr Gully, was causing an expansion of the remote little village into a spa town. Facilities for well-to-do visitors burgeoned, and the lady of the manor presided over building development with enthusiasm – and greater efficiency than many a later planning committee. She was widely respected but in her later years was mocked for her love of status: in 1869 the editor of the *Malvern News* scoffed at her revival of manorial courts as 'bustling, silly exhibitions.' Undoubtedly she enjoyed a bit of a show. At the age of ninety-two she went to Hereford Shire Hall clad in a scarlet satin gown and white bonnet trimmed with red and blue ribbons for the unveiling of Queen Victoria's diamond jubilee portrait. It is a pity that no picture is available of Lady Foley herself in this gloriously patriotic attire.

---

8.   C. F. Severn Burrow, *A Little City Set on a Hill,* p.84.

9.   Ibid.

She was reputed to be a good employer, providing above average cottages for her workers, who were expected to keep them in good condition. Paying low rents, they were also expected to keep their gardens well stocked, thus producing food for their families. She gave generously to the church, donating land for numerous new churches and schools, which she continued to support with money and by regular inspections of them.

More controversially, she used ancient manorial rights to allow considerable encroachment which men like Stephen Ballard,

Stoke Edith Park, Herefordshire.

This early nineteenth century drawing of Stoke Edith House appeared in Mary Southall's *Description of Malvern*. Southall's guide included several examples, such as this one, of the work of the lithographer I. Bradley.

the Colwall engineer and protector of ordinary men and women, considered to be 'pilfering of the common land.' They had a convincing case since the Foley estate benefited from payments, known as acknowledgements, demanded from encroachers while commoners lost valuable rights over land that thus fell into private ownership. Lady Foley, however, actually had substantial historic rights and, whatever others may have felt about, for example, the modest homes built in the Newtown Road and Link Top area, she was breaking no laws. At the other end of the social scale, the new

Graham Road of the 1850s, honouring for all time her own family name, contained the most desirable new houses on large building plots with restrictive covenants to prevent any lowering of the tone, though it might be added that she allowed much of the commercial property in Church Street to deteriorate.

She was also patron of eight benefices with the right to appoint their clergy. These included Great Malvern Priory Church and Holy Trinity at Link Top. Miss Severn Burrow, born in 1871, recalled her father as churchwarden of Great Malvern Priory Church leading Lady

The west front of Stoke Edith House in the early twentieth century. Seriously damaged by fire in 1927, it was eventually demolished, despite efforts to conserve part of it.

Foley up the main aisle of the nave to her usual reserved seat in the monks' stalls in the choir. Miss Severn Burrow confirms Lady Foley's love of rich clothes, describing her 'rich be-bustled gown with short train, and a bugled purple mantle, surmounted by the most amazing bonnet covered with flowers and high ostrich tips, with broad mauve strings tied at one side.'[10]

In 1888, her ladyship sent a telegram to her ten-year-old great-nephew – later the sixth Duke of Montrose – instructing him to pay her a visit at Stoke Edith. Given firm warnings by his mother as to how he should

10. Ibid.

The last picture of Lady Emily Foley,
taken on 7 December 1899, less than a month before she died.
Courtesy Humphrey Bartleet.

behave, he nervously set off by train and was welcomed at Hereford station by 'a tall footman in silver-buttoned great-coat, with white powdered hair and cockaded tall hat.' Outside was the locally famous yellow carriage emblazoned with the Foley coat of arms and drawn by two horses on one of which was a liveried postilion, wearing – like the accompanying outrider – a wig and a peaked cap. The tall footman put the boy's luggage in another vehicle and stood on a platform at the back of the carriage for the journey to Stoke Edith. Great-aunt Emily was seated in an armchair at the top of the steps by the front door and introduced him to various members of the household, some of whom had prepared his bedroom, following her instructions to lay out numerous gifts suitable for a young boy, including a model of the Tudor ship, the *Great Harry*. During his stay, at successive dinners, carefully minding his manners, he was impressed by her ladyship's upright bearing and 'wonderful décolleté gowns of superb material.' She also wore 'marvellous jewels.' The choice varied: it might be 'all sapphires, all emeralds, all rubies or all diamonds.' Sunday morning and church attendance had a drama all its own:

> … when the bells began to ring we formed up in procession with the tall footman leading, carrying a purple cushion upon which were laid Aunt Emily's Bible and Prayer Book. Behind the footman walked my aunt in black silk crinoline dress and wearing a poke bonnet, and she led me by the hand. We had a full choral service and a long address by the Dean of Hereford. After church the procession wound its way home through beautiful formal gardens.[11]

The Duke of Montrose wrote his autobiography in *My Ditty Box* – a reference to the box used by sailors to store their precious personal papers and other possessions. Writing about his Stoke Edith experience over sixty years later, he recognised that the whole set up seems stilted to the modern mind but 'we must recollect Great-Aunt Emily was living naturally as she had always done during the lives of

---

11. James Graham, *My Ditty Box*, p.21–23.

four sovereigns, and I feel I was fortunate to have witnessed, at first hand, the old customs of long ago.'

This grand old lady died, according to the *Malvern Advertiser* of 6 January 1900, 'of the prevailing epidemic' in the early hours of 1 January 1900 – her sense of timing impeccable as ever. Her epitaph was added to the imposing monument in Stoke Edith Church erected to her husband over fifty years previously. One wonders if she chose it herself: 'Think upon me, my God, for good, according to all that I have done for this people.' (Nehemiah 5:19). It certainly reflected the love and respect – doubtless tinged with quiet mirth at her love of splendour– in which she was held. Like Lady Lyttelton, she was the product of her class: their sense of entitlement to privilege and respect was balanced by their sense of obligation to provide for the less fortunate. Egalitarian they certainly were not.

Lady Howard de Walden (1806–1899)

Lady Howard De Walden was born in 1806 the fourth daughter and last survivor of William Henry Cavendish Bentinck, fourth Duke of Portland. Named Lucy Joan Scott Cavendish, she married in November 1828 Charles Augustus, sixth Baron de Walden, who became the British Minister at Brussels and died in 1868. Of their numerous offspring the eldest son, born in 1830, became seventh baron at that time and his mother lived a widow for another thirty-one years, so like Lady Lyttelton and Lady Foley, she spent a large part of her life without a husband to overshadow her. She was, however, much richer than they.

Indeed, she was immensely rich, her main properties being in Marylebone and southern Scotland. One obituary stated that:

> Lady Howard de Walden was the richest, and perhaps the most eccentric, woman in Great Britain. She inherited all the London property of her brother the fifth Duke of Portland when he died in 1879 and, though that was but a part of his vast estates, possibly it was the best portion ... he died worth about £17 million.

She also inherited property from other siblings who pre-deceased her.

Although she probably spent about £100,000 on her West Malvern home and estate it was only one of her homes and she spent less than ten years in it. She extended and beautified the mid-nineteenth-century house and the figure of £100,000 – an enormous sum in the nineteenth century – is probably accurate when one recalls what was written about it in 1902 when the Baird sisters acquired it to accommodate St James School.

Lady Howard de Walden, who spent a fortune on St James' House in the 1890s.
Courtesy Malvern St James.

We come at last to St James's. Surely unique buildings and occupying a most noble site. A great cluster of pale Cradley stone raised on cloisters, or rather loggias, with steps and balustrades leading to different levels. Inside, rooms of space and proportion, with mantel-pieces carved in the classic manner, inset with coloured marble and Wedgewood medallions. The great windows look westwards to the hills of Wales, a breathtaking, inexhaustible view; golden, outstretched with shadowed woods and lesser valleys … The gardens, which they said employed seventy gardeners to make, stretch along the hillside, planted with groves and vistas, shrubs and trees that Kew might envy. Terraces and stairways, rose temples and grass walks and little dripping streams.[12]

Lady Howard de Walden also spent money on mock timber-

---

12. Alice Baird, *I Was There,* p.17, comment of Nancy Campbell.

framed buildings including Model Farm (the farmland itself is now Runnings Park).

She died at the mansion on 29 July 1899 aged ninety-two and was cremated at the new crematorium in Woking: at that time cremation was a novel method of dealing with the deceased. In its obituary the *Daily Telegraph* commented that she was:

> ... a woman of exceptional intellectual powers and of brilliant and original wit. Her charities were unbounded, and every philanthropic scheme or movement for increasing the enjoyment of the people found in her a generous supporter. Her benevolence was exercised in a quiet and unostentatious manner.

Her widespread benevolence included £10,000 to erect the National Dental Hospital and College in London's Great Portland Street and substantial donations to the Prince of Wales Hospital Fund, to the Howard de Walden Institute at Maidstone in Kent, to the Church of England Schools in Eastbourne and to Marylebone High School for Girls. Locally, in 1893 she paid over £400 to sort out the sanitation at West Malvern National Schools, made contributions to the Malvern Hills Conservators and spent about £4,000 on paths on the Malverns to make the hills more accessible. The *Malvern Advertiser* wrote that:

> The gossips say that when she was driving over the hills she would suddenly get the idea that she would want to go by a certain route, and when she was told that she could not do so because there was no road in this route, she would order a road to be made at her expense in the lordliest way.

When the Malvern Hills Conservators were founded in 1884 her generosity in this somewhat majestic provision of hill paths was acknowledged.

This was certainly a lady with a sense of social responsibility, coupled with a sense of entitlement and a habit of getting her own way.

Lady Henry Somerset (1851–1921)

A very different manner was adopted by Lady Henry Somerset. She spent time as a child and young woman a few miles from Malvern at Eastnor Castle and from 1883 was its owner. It was part of the extensive estates of the Somers-Cocks family: her great-grandfather, John Somers-Cocks, first Earl Somers, had built the castle in the early nineteenth century; his wife was Margaret, daughter of Worcestershire's highly respected historian, the Revd Treadway Russell Nash. The highly valuable collection of antiquarian books accumulated by Nash came to Eastnor Castle after his 1811 death. Isabel[la] Somers-Cocks, born in 1851, was the eldest of the three daughters of the young third Earl Somers and his wife, who was the sister of the pioneer photographer Julia Margaret Cameron. Lady Isabel had some interesting role models in her family.

At the age of twenty Isabel married Lord Henry Somerset, son of one of the county's leading noblemen – the Duke of Beaufort. The bridegroom seemed to be quite a charmer but, although they had a son in 1874, the marriage was obviously very unhappy from its earliest days and they were separated after seven years, when she was in her late twenties. Interestingly both her parents-in-law sympathised with her, the Duchess of Beaufort writing to her in 1877 of their shame at their son's behaviour:

> You have always been most kind in trying to screen Penna from the very natural and just wrath of your Father and Mother at the treatment you receive at his hands … We have nothing whatever to say in defence of Penna and unless he is mad cannot understand his behaviour. Be quite sure of this you dear that nothing can ever make any difference in our great affection for you. If you were our own child we could not love you more, and whatever altered circumstances Penna's conduct may bring about, you must always look upon this as your second Home, and believe that you are as welcome a sight to us as you have always been. 'She is the sunshine of our house' the Duke always says, and all the boys feel the same … We are bitterly grieved and ashamed that anyone belonging to us should treat you as Penna has.[13]

The Duke told his son to pull himself together, 'Isabel's conduct is irreproachable ... You will never get the child in any court of law – a man may get tired of his wife but your conduct and language is not that of a gentleman.'[14]

Lady Isabel left her home and took her son, Henry Charles Somers Augustus Somerset, to the care of her own parents, thus putting herself legally in the wrong – in the nineteenth century wives and offspring were rated as a husband's property so fathers' rights were supreme. Astonishingly, when her husband applied to have his son returned to him in May 1878 Mr Justice Field risked the wrath of the Beauforts and public criticism by awarding custody to the wife, despite the legal technicalities. The Beaufort connection was, however, also maintained – he was to be brought up as a member of the Beaufort family not just as a Somers-Cocks.

Nineteenth-century coyness about the reason for the marriage ending in a legal separation, caused one young woman to refer to something 'that was only mentioned in the Bible.' In fact, Lord Henry Somerset not only preferred the company of young men but also spent his wife's money on his homosexual lovers. She was also the one to pay the social price of the marriage breakdown: despite her parents and friends supporting her, she was cut by society, while the husband of a friend told her, 'Of course I understand that you are in the right but you must not mind my wife not knowing you, because I could not explain to her.'[15]

Charming, kind and sympathetic to anyone in trouble, she lived an outwardly happy life at her family's property the Priory in Reigate, attending parties and balls, but she had been deeply hurt. When her father, Lord Somers, died in 1883 she went to live at Eastnor Castle where for the next seven years she looked after the estate and visited the poor. In 1887 she was despondent, after two years of living virtually alone in what she described in her diary as 'unbroken monotony'.[16] Stephen Ballard of Colwall kept

---

13. Kathleen Fitzpatrick, *Lady Henry Somerset*, p.100.

14. Ibid, p.101.

15. Ibid, p.107.

a news-cutting book containing a comment on her seeking solitude, 'educating her boy, adored by her domestics, but seeing few visitors; working out for herself, step by step, the duty to which she was called.'

She valued the trust and affection of those she helped, but missed her old society, which still made malicious comment about her. Even her attempts to improve the life of her tenants caused adverse comment: one gentleman claimed she had 'disfigured the country with new cottages.'

Lady Henry Somerset,
née Lady Isabella Somers-Cocks.

Her concern for the poor became intertwined with her craving to be a true Christian and she supported a temperance group in Ledbury, three miles from her Eastnor home. She herself enjoyed alcohol but believed, if she recommended others to give it up, she must do so herself. There is a story of her taking her last glass of port at Worcester Station refreshment room on her return from London the day before the meeting at Eastnor when she and her household would sign the pledge never to drink alcohol again. A Methodist group in Ledbury did its best to help the inhabitants of the teeming hovels of Ledbury's Bye Street and, despite criticism from the church and upper classes, she set up Missions at Hollybush, Castlemorton as well as in Bye Street, providing in Bye Street converted clowns and other attractions to make temperance popular. Like the story of a last drink in the less than enticing location of a station refreshment room, there is here an almost amusing naivety about her efforts to do the right thing in circumstances where she must have felt awkward,

---

16. Ibid, p.122.

The Somers-Cocks Herefordshire home, Eastnor Castle, in the early twentieth century.

out of her depth and surrounded by critics. An impudent young curate actually criticised her actions from the pulpit of Eastnor Church where she was one of the congregation. Due to the fact that she claimed that 'unspeakable drudgery' had led to the immorality of the working classes, she was confronted with the accusation that she was a traitor to her class. She felt that her class might be traitors to their fellow countrymen, finding it difficult to see as Christian a society in which the upper classes lived in comfort while others lived in abject poverty.

She was tireless in her encouragement of Bible reading – often in the homes of farmers on the Eastnor estate. At Eastnor Castle she held mothers' meetings, and her support for temperance added power to the elbow of people like Maria Ballard, who with her daughters organised the Band of Hope in Colwall.

In the knowledge of her perception of the injustice in a supposedly Christian country, it is not surprising to find that, despite her class, she actively supported trade unionism when the success of the Dockers' Strike of 1889 demonstrated that unskilled workers by combining together could challenge and actually triumph over employers who, until then, always held the trump cards. Her concern and first-hand knowledge about working-class conditions also meant that she had particular sympathy with women and the disadvantages they endured. Their wages were even lower than men's for very long hours of hard manual work. On top of this many coped with frequent pregnancies and the demands of family responsibilities so their lot was often even harder than that of men.

As she grew more confident her work for the temperance movement took her to America and led to a close association with Frances Willard who was a leading light in the movement in the United States. By 1893 the British Women's Temperance Association had extended its work to 'the oversight of all branches of moral, social and political reform which are radically connected with the cause of Temperance' – a very broad spectrum indeed, and one which led to considerable, by no means entirely favourable, publicity.

The last eighteen years of her life were spent in trying to alleviate the problems of women whose lives had been ruined by drunkenness. In Duxhurst, near her home at Reigate Priory in Surrey, she had in the 1890s set up a Colony for Women Inebriates, where the women grew fruit and vegetables, with mixed results concerning their ability to overcome their weakness for strong drink.

She died in March 1921 at the age of sixty-nine.

Two Beauchamp Ladies
There were several Lady Beauchamps in the nineteenth century and the one who probably made the most lasting impression was unaware that she had done so. She was Charlotte, wife of the third Earl: she had the idea of erecting almshouses to provide homes for long-serving staff when they became too elderly or infirm to continue in service at Madresfield Court. Although the almshouses were not built until some years after her 1846 death, her husband, nicknamed 'the peasants' earl' for his generosity to his less wealthy neighbours, wanted the almshouses to be a memorial to her but he died in 1853 before the work could be carried out. Eventually, in the 1860s, the sixth earl, a deeply religious man, included them in his building plans: a new church at Newland, dedicated to St Leonard, replaced the modest (and remarkably well-preserved) medieval church and, with the almshouses, formed an impressive neo-Gothic collegiate-

Madresfield Court, home of the Beauchamps.

style complex of buildings, all of which still stand. The original purpose is no longer appropriate but the Beauchamp Community, as it became known, continues to provide sheltered accommodation for elderly men and women, especially communicant members of the Church of England.

In the twentieth century the life of another Lady Beauchamp had even greater effect on Malvern and its environs. She was Else Schiwe, Danish-born in 1895, who married the eighth earl in 1936 as her second husband. They had no children, though she had a child from her first marriage. During the Second World War she and her husband faced the task of preparing their home at Madresfield Court for the reception of the royal family if it became necessary for them to leave London, an eventuality which fortunately did not happen. Remembered by friends and family for her enthusiasm and *joie de vivre,* she rode her tricycle round the grounds of Madresfield well into old age.

Her public service was remarkable: honoured for her wartime work with the Women's Voluntary Service (MBE) and her work for the St John Ambulance Brigade (DBE), she also gave support to the Red Cross and to movements concerned with girls and women.[17] She

---

17. Dorothy Williams, *The Lygons of Madresfield Court,* p.123.

St Leonard's Church and the Beauchamp almshouses,
built in Newland in the late nineteenth century as a result of Beauchamp family
concern for their elderly staff at Madresfield Court and estate.

valued the contributions made by Girl Guides and Women's Institutes, recognising the important part they can play in the country's social and economic life.

When the earl died in 1979 she was the main beneficiary of his Madresfield effects and, before her own death in 1989, put her mind to securing a continuation of the family's tradition of sponsoring the arts. This led her to endow the Elmley Foundation, which takes its name from the title by which her husband was known until he inherited the earldom in 1938. Directed from its inception by her grandson, John de la Cour, it makes generous contributions to festivals such as those held for the Three Choirs and for Hay-on-Wye, as well as to the Autumn in Malvern Festival. Lady Beauchamp's legacy has proved highly significant in encouraging art, craft and design in Worcestershire and Herefordshire.

ECONOMIC CONTRIBUTIONS
MADE BY WOMEN TO MALVERN

Mary Southall

Mary Southall was the wife of the organist at Great Malvern Priory Church. She and her husband kept the Library and Reading Room at the junction of Edith Walk with the main Worcester Road. Built in the early nineteenth century as part of Edward Foley's scheme to beautify his manor of Malvern, the Library became the Royal Library as a result of royal visitors, such as the young Princess Victoria, and enhanced the approach into Malvern from Worcester. It subsequently became one of Barclays Bank's more architecturally impressive branches.

Mary Southall left a remarkable legacy in her *Description of Malvern* first published in 1822, with numerous later 1820s editions, and providing a vivid portrait of what was in her time still little more than a village – but appears to have been a village with inhabitants who had aspirations to greater things. The similarities between her work and John Chambers' 1817 *A General History of Malvern* show her as an unashamed plagiarist but her books are of immeasurable interest to all who are interested in the history of Malvern.

Boarding House Keepers

Nineteenth-century Malvern had boarding houses which became more numerous as the water-cure caught on. Some were kept by women such as Eliza Partington of Montreal House in the Worcester Road, where in 1851 Charles Darwin's beloved daughter Anne

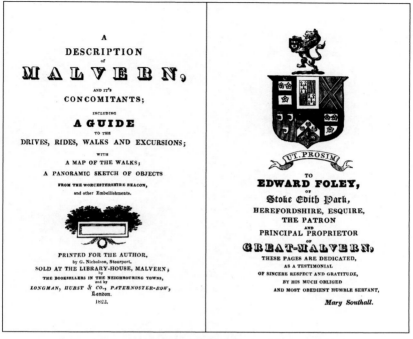

A

DESCRIPTION

of

MALVERN,

AND IT's

CONCOMITANTS;

INCLUDING

A GUIDE

TO THE

DRIVES, RIDES, WALKS AND EXCURSIONS;

WITH

A MAP OF THE WALKS;

A PANORAMIC SKETCH OF OBJECTS

FROM THE WORCESTERSHIRE BEACON,

and other Embellishments.

PRINTED FOR THE AUTHOR,

by G. Nicholson, Stourport.

SOLD AT THE LIBRARY-HOUSE, MALVERN;

by

THE BOOKSELLERS IN THE NEIGHBOURING TOWNS,

and by

LONGMAN, HURST & CO., PATERNOSTER-ROW,

London.

1822.

UT. PROSIM

TO

EDWARD FOLEY,

OF

Stoke Edith Park,

HEREFORDSHIRE, ESQUIRE,

THE PATRON

AND

PRINCIPAL PROPRIETOR

OF

GREAT-MALVERN,

THESE PAGES ARE DEDICATED,

AS A TESTIMONIAL

OF SINCERE RESPECT AND GRATITUDE,

BY HIS MUCH OBLIGED

AND MOST OBEDIENT HUMBLE SERVANT,

Mary Southall.

The title page of Mary Southall's *Description of Malvern* was followed by a dedication to Edward Foley, lord of the manor of Malvern.

Elizabeth died of tuberculosis and from where her body was taken for burial in Great Malvern Priory churchyard. Mrs Matthews, born in 1866 in Lanarkshire, kept Malvern House, the Misses Dowding let out apartments in Trafalgar House, next to the Foley Arms Hotel and other such women owned or worked in establishments and earned a living from meeting the needs of visitors.

Donkey Women

One particularly colourful group was that of donkey women. By the middle of the century they – and perhaps even more their donkeys and juvenile employees – were kept busy by visitors keen to hire a donkey to take them up the Malvern Hills. Cuthbert Bede – the pen-name of the Revd Edward Bradley – assumed the identity of a disgruntled old man visiting Malvern for the first time in thirty years

Library & Boarding House

An illustration from Southall's *Description of Malvern* showing the Royal Library
(named in honour of Princess Victoria's visit when people queued to catch a glimpse of her).

and recorded his impressions with particular mention of the donkeys, which he considered to be among 'the unalterable fixtures of the place' so sadly, in his view, changed in other respects. He wrote an article describing the scene in Malvern on 11 July 1861 when the celebrated Blondin attracted large crowds as he walked a tightrope near to Pickersleigh House. Bede thought the donkeys were 'thwacked' more than necessary, and had his suspicions about 'pins being somewhat too freely used in connection with the extremities of the donkey and the driver's stick,' but 'I am glad to say that the donkeys are well cared for.'[1] They were well fed with three feeds a day of oats, beans, bran and chaff plus a bit of hay when stabled at night, as well as snatched grazing on their way down from the top of the hills. A donkey boy claimed that on a particularly busy day he and his donkey went up and down hill about ten times, and even the donkey women might

1.   Cuthbert Bede, 'Malvern Donkeys,' *Leisure Hour* (1862).

Down's Hotel.

The hotel kept by John Down and later named
the Foley Arms in honour of the lord of the manor of Malvern.

do the journey eight times. The donkey proprietors, 'generally of the softer sex, who drive the hardest bargains,' did not pay the boys and girls who worked for them but gave them board and lodging, any payment being given in the form of gratuities by those who hired them. But they were well fed, 'the missuses does us very well and gives us the best of vittles.' Donkeys, usually with side saddles, were hired by women and children for a fee of about 9*d* or a shilling (5*p*) if the young driver could get it, while men liked to hire mules, which cost twice the price. A few of the donkeys had panniers 'for those little trots who cannot be trusted to hold on to the pommels; and for these double-barrelled donkeys double price is charged.' Proprietors had to pay five shillings for an annual licence, keeping their animals at the main donkey stations at Victoria Drive and at Winding Valley between North Hill and the Worcestershire Beacon, where sixty donkeys, four mules and two ponies were based. There were also private stables and smaller stations at Malvern Link, Malvern Wells and West Malvern.

The redoubtable Betty Caley, one of the donkey women who liked to wear a red cloak, is probably the person at the front of this group of donkey women, holding her donkey, Royal Moses. Young Princess Victoria preferred to ride a donkey called Moses when she visited Malvern so he acquired the adjective 'royal'. Reputedly, his oldest descendants were honoured with the same name: there are many stories, doubtless embellished over the years, about the donkeys and their proprietors.

Some Shopkeepers

Cuthbert Bede's article also refers to 'that old lady at the Abbey Gateway, who (now in her eighty-sixth year) presides over game and green-grocery, and still announces herself as "Sausage-maker to her Royal Highness the Duchess of Kent"' – a reference to old Mrs Clay who supplied her sausages to the royal visitors when the young Princess Victoria and her mother, the Duchess of Kent, stayed at Holly Mount over thirty years earlier.

Many of Malvern's growing body of retailers were women, especially those keeping shops of particular appeal to women. Malvern's largest and grandest store was Warwick House, a department store in the Wells Road founded in the 1830s by George Warwick and transformed into apartments after one hundred and seventy years of trading. Smaller shops also offered clothes for ladies and children and an extensive selection of goods needed for feminine arts and crafts such as embroidery. The proprietors of these were often women, as shown in a late nineteenth-century edition of a guide as to *Where to Buy in Malvern.*

Miss Pullen kept the Berlin Wool, Art Needlework and Fancy Repository at 8, the Promenade. The entry for her gives a nineteenth-century flavour to recreational hobbies for well-bred ladies, as well as some questionable opinions on the differences between men and women:

> Art needlework is essentially a lady's accomplishment ... The beauties of nature do not attract the male mind in the same degree as the female; the latter are more demonstrative about them, and draw greater enjoyment from their presence ... A favourite house in Malvern for the purchase of Berlin wools and specialities in needlework is that of Miss Pullen, of 8 Promenade. Miss Pullen's business was formerly carried on at Belle Vue Terrace adjacent to the Belle Vue Hotel, but the premises being required for the erection of a new bank, she has removed to her present handsome premises in the Promenade and near the Post Office in the main Worcester Road. Miss Pullen has made ladies' requirements in this direction a study; Berlin wool is one of the principal features, and the selection embraces a wonderful assortment of beautiful shades and textures. A great variety of tea cloths and table centres is also kept in stock; silks for embroidery with newest designs for mantel borders, antimacassars, sofa cushions etc are here in abundance. Ladies' own work is mounted, according to any required design, and a selection of designs for mounting is kept, from which a choice may be made. All kinds of knitting wools, fingerings, Shetlands, as well as many fancy embroideries, and every description of art needlework can be obtained here ... At this establishment there is also a pretty display of decorative articles in bric-a-brac, fancy goods, etc.

Mrs F. Jones, Hatter, Hosier, Glover and Boys' Outfitter at Canton House, Church Street had a rather broader appeal:

The premises are situated in Church Street ... A special feature is made of boys' clothing, and the department contains a complete selection of man-o'-war suits, including lanyards, whistle, doublets etc in serge, cashmere, velvets and washing materials in all sizes, and at all prices; boys' tweed knicker suits, and in short everything of service for juvenile wear. Regulation and Eton suits are made to order ... Experienced workmen are kept on the premises, and ... are always busy executing orders ... The various branches contain extensive

The Belle Vue Hotel by Bradley.

and well-selected stocks of gloves, shirts, collars, hosiery and ties, the many goods which contribute to the completeness of a gentleman's wardrobe. Special attention is paid to the men's and boys' hats in silk, felt, straw etc. This is the local depot for the celebrated seamless hosiery, which is made extra stout for school wear, every size of boys' and youths' undershirts and drawers being kept ... Shirts made to measure are worthy of special mention and, in ordering, gentlemen may confidently depend upon obtaining a combination of perfect fit, superior material and well-finished workmanship. Dressing gowns, travelling bags, silk and other hats, umbrellas and various other goods are on hand, and ...everything is guaranteed of the best quality procurable.

Miss E. M. Baylis, bookseller and stationer on Belle Vue Terrace, prided herself on being able to supply the needs of an intellectual clientele:

> The Christian Knowledge Society have made this shop their depot, and all their publications are to be found here, besides many other works of a religious or semi-religious character which in their neat or handsome bindings are very attractive to those whose tastes lead them to prefer solid and instructive literature to the lighter and more ephemeral productions of the day ... The assortment of stationery is equal to all demands ... Birthday, text and other cards form an attractive feature ... hand-painted illuminations ... of a very superior character as regards design and execution.

From about 1876 Mrs H. E. Guy kept the Fancy Goods and Stationery Stores at Paris House, opposite the Priory Church, Church Street (the shop, later trading as Camerons, was still meeting similar needs until the latter part of the twentieth century, when it moved to a site lower down Church Street which subsequently became the St Michael's Hospice Charity shop):

> Purses, albums, writing and letter cases, pocket books, note books and diaries are kept in great variety; court note paper and envelopes, in all the newest and most fashionable styles and shapes; correspondence, menu and visiting cards, besides every kind of fancy stationery, have all been purchased from the very best wholesale houses with due regard to their quality and utility. Views of and guides to Malvern and the Worcestershire and Herefordshire Beacons may be obtained

here and ...vases, china and glass goods in variety, Japanese oddities ... It is always pleasant to bring away some tangible reminiscence from a place where an enjoyable holiday has been spent, and from Mrs Guy's stock it will be an easy matter to select a souvenir ... of one of the most delightful spots in all England.

Such shopkeepers would have benefited from the influx of water-cure patients and other visitors to the delights of Malvern. Census returns describe some working-class women as *bathwomen,* showing that the water-cure which caused the growth of Malvern offered work in the hydropathic establishments run by men such as Dr Wilson and Dr Gully, the pioneers of water treatment in Malvern, and other doctors who followed them to set up fashionable and lucrative practices. Other work would have included all kinds of domestic positions as cleaners, cooks and kitchen maids.

Pioneering Schoolmistresses

Other women sought to provide the daughters of the well-to-do with an education that would enable them to manage the households of the men they married or – if that career, highly desired by most girls and their parents, did not materialise – to become financially self-sufficient in an age when the subservient role of women was changing. Some changes were brought about by a gradually growing perception that women were entitled to rights such as the right to vote, but some were brought about by the cataclysmic effects of the First World War. In the relatively short-term it caused women to take on the work – which they did remarkably well - of men away fighting. But more permanent change resulted from the premature deaths of so many young men: it became obvious that statistically many women could have no man – father, husband or brother – to support them financially so that the nineteenth-century financial dependence of women on men simply could not continue.

Several women founded girls' schools which established high and lasting reputations – a distinct cut above the numerous little schools for small boys and girls in the nineteenth-century homes of people who themselves sometimes had few, if any, qualifications or talents to fit them for the work. Those women who truly succeeded in the educational field by the closing years of the nineteenth century were obviously in competition with each other – private education is, after all, a business. They also, however, faced the same challenges and shared certain characteristics which enabled them to achieve their objectives: they were competent, diligent and shrewd, recognising a market that they could satisfy and showing a strength of purpose too often believed to have been found only in men.

Founders of Malvern Girls' College, Isabel Greenslade (left) and Lily Poulton (right) flanking the charismatic Blanche Mitchell, who was a principal at Malvern Girls' College from 1902–1917.
Courtesy Malvern St James.

Lily Poulton and Isabel Greenslade were two such ladies. They were friends who in 1893 founded a small school for boys and girls in the front room of the Poulton family home in College Road. It must have seemed indistinguishable from all the other little schools Malvern had seen. But it was not. Miss Poulton had a good brain for business and Miss Greenslade was a trained teacher: the combination led to the rapid rise of their school. Within seven years they gave

Alice Baird who founded St James School.
Courtesy Malvern St James.

up accepting boys, took over an existing school for young ladies and, most unusually for the early twentieth century, offered a broad range of education up to university entrance level for the daughters of those who could afford the fees. Their shrewd grasp of market realities meant that they were able to offer the kind of education that enabled pupils to become professional women, with professional salaries, at a time when many intelligent women would never have the opportunity for the career which most middle-class women had seen as their likely, and preferred, lot in life – marriage.[2] The Poulton and Greenslade creation became Malvern Girls' College, flourished and eventually amalgamated in 2006 with St James' School, another girls' school with a commitment to high standards. The amalgamated school is the present Malvern St James, housed in the former Imperial Hotel which Malvern Girls' College had bought in 1919.

The seeds of St James had been sown in 1896 by the Baird twins, Katrine and Alice, who later came to Malvern and seized upon Lady Howard de Walden's former home, St James House, with the same vigour and enthusiasm as that with which Miss Poulton and Miss Greenslade gobbled up considerable property in the Avenue Road area of Malvern. Upper class and born in 1871, the mid Victorian period, the twins had five sisters. All (except Constance who, after sterling work nursing and driving in a France devastated by the First World War, started a poultry farm and bred cocker spaniels in nearby Welland) became deeply involved in girls' education. One sister

2.   Pamela Hurle, *Malvern Girls' College.*

remarked, 'We were too tall to get married, so what else could we do?'[3] They visited and taught in numerous schools before founding their own, and the twins also spent some time at Newnham College, Cambridge, though this was before women could take degrees in Oxford and Cambridge. With the encouragement of their father they started a school in 1896 at Southbourne near Christchurch in Hampshire, moving to Crowborough in Sussex after four years. They had one pupil in their first term and three in their second. From such modest beginnings they moved to Malvern in 1902, leasing the St James estate until they eventually purchased it in 1924. In 1912 Katrine went to take charge of Abbot's Hill School, which still flourishes near Hemel Hempstead, whilst Alice, assisted by her sister Diana as housemistress, was principal at St James until 1948, having been running a school for over fifty years. The family also set up a trust in 1933 to take responsibility for Evendine Court in Colwall. This college for domestic studies originally founded in 1886 by Mrs Buck and Miss Brander was to be run by Georgina Baird. Mary Baird, kind and deeply religious, was a trained musician who worked at both St James and Abbot's Hill, until her sudden death in 1927. Helena, secretary to the headmaster of Eton, died from pneumonia in 1908.

The success of such schools owed much to the foundations laid down by members of that indefatigable breed of Victorian ladies, unusual in their vision and blessed with common sense and good business brains. The Bairds had the added advantage of social contact with upper-class families who had an interest in educating their daughters, as well as the money to enable them to afford to do so.

The Abbey School for girls moved to Malvern Link in 1897, having been founded in 1880 not far away in Blockley by the widowed Margaret Judson. Her daughters, Florence and Alice, took over when the school came to Malvern, soon moving to a more impressive site in Malvern Wells. The Judson ladies headed the school until 1942. Eventually the Abbey, one of the first of the pioneering Malvern girls' schools to suffer from declining numbers

---

3.　Kate Chester-Lamb, *Eventful Days,* p.12.

Unlike Malvern College, founded for boys in 1865, girls' schools lacked financial backers and, as funds became available, made use of existing buildings which they often leased and sometimes managed to buy. Malvern Girls' College bought the ailing Imperial Hotel in 1919 when its German-born proprietor, Friedrich Moerschall, was unpopular because of the First World War. This card suggests that he gave up active management – he may actually have been interned, despite having taken British citizenship and the name Frederick Marshall in the late nineteenth century.

as the popularity of boarding and single-sex schools declined, merged with St James in 1979.

St James in fact proved to be particularly successful as it also absorbed, in 1994, Lawnside, which was at that time the oldest girls' school in Malvern: it may even have been the Seminary for young ladies mentioned in the 1820s by Mary Southall as 'at a short distance from the village, where Young Ladies are instructed in every branch of polite and useful education by the Misses Billings.' The first firmly established facts are that in the 1850s Miss Caroline Cooper, granddaughter of a French *émigré* who came to England after the French Revolution, ran a school for young ladies in Malvern Wells, moving to various sites in Malvern.[4] In the 1870s Miss Janet Leighton, one of a succession of formidable headmistresses, took over the school and in 1884 moved it to Lawnside, the house at the junction of Avenue Road and Albert Road South: this gave the school the name by which it was known for the rest of its life. Like Miss Poulton, she was also breaking new ground in working very actively to set up a School of Art, which eventually materialised in 1891.[5] In 1925 a remarkable principal, who was a former head girl of the school, took over and ruled Lawnside for the next thirty-five years, including the period of

This view of West Malvern shows the prominent St James' building, set in delightful grounds. Once the home of Lady Howard de Walden, it was subsequently occupied by St James' School for over a hundred years.

the almost magical pre-war Malvern Festivals, when famous actors, writers and artists like Dame Laura Knight were entertained at the house and in its delightful gardens. This principal was Miss Winifred Barrows, a woman similar in character to her contemporary Miss Iris Brooks who was head at Malvern Girls' College from 1928 until 1954. Both were strong and opinionated, and both worked wonders for the

4.   Mary Dixey, Duseline Stewart, and Sheila Barker, *Lawnside: The History of a Malvern School*.

5.   Fray, 'Artistic Community in Late Victorian Malvern'.

reputations of their schools. Their views of each other are not clear but would certainly be interesting.

Another successful founder was Miss Gladys Sayle who set up a school in Bushey and brought it to Ellerslie House in Malvern in 1922. She retained ownership until 1955, when a trust took over, eventually merging the school in 1991 with Malvern College which, founded as a boys' public school in 1865, was taking its first steps into full co-education.

All these women had deep and lasting effects in Malvern and, as their students left to take up careers, marry and raise families, the effects spread into the wider world. As with some of Malvern's aristocratic ladies, the town's founding mothers of female education were neither helped nor hindered by husbands. Their achievements

Lawnside hosted numerous parties during the 1930s Malvern Festivals.
Dame Laura Knight is at the right-hand side of the middle row, and her husband is half-hidden in the back row. George Bernard Shaw sits in the middle of the front row and the Festival promoter, Barry Jackson, is on the right.
Courtesy Malvern St James.

were the result of their own ambition, drive and hard work. They were not content to accept the conventional role of seen-but-not-heard middle-class Victorian ladies; their equally shrewd successors likewise saw the business and social potential of the devastating effects of war and politics in the first half of the twentieth century.

The demise of the individual girls' schools in the late twentieth and early twenty-first centuries reflected not only parents' doubts about sending their offspring to boarding schools but also society's move towards co-education. Boys' schools saw many advantages to be gained from admitting girls, and the girls' schools which had done so much for women's emancipation felt the draughts of social and economic reality. Those shrewd female pioneers in girls' education had, nevertheless, helped to achieve that significant phenomenon – the right of girls to receive an education equal to that of their brothers. Many parents today still believe that single sex education can be most beneficial for girls, not least because it avoids pressure generated by gender to study, for example, arts rather than scientific subjects. Perhaps, one day, such schools will again become a beacon for a return to earlier practices – a notion worth considering despite the controversy ever present in educational circles.

Schools such as those mentioned have long made a significant impact on employment opportunities for domestic workers, housemen and groundsmen as well as academic and administrative staff. Local shops providing groceries, uniforms and many other types of merchandise also benefit substantially from their regular orders and from purchases by parents, many of whom used also to seek accommodation in the town's hotels and boarding houses. Education has been, and remains, an important part of Malvern's economy.

WOMEN WHO MADE
CULTURAL CONTRIBUTIONS

Elizabeth Barrett Browning (1806–1861)
The life of Elizabeth Barrett Browning has been well documented by many authors and she did not return to live here in the area where she spent twenty-three of her formative years – she reputedly likened a return to trying to return a plucked flower to the plant. Nevertheless, Malvern can lay claim to her as one of its daughters, living nearby at Hope End, near Ledbury until her mid twenties, having been brought here by her parents in 1809 when she was three years old. Her father replaced the seventeenth-century house at the Hope End estate with an unusual eastern style building topped by minarets and surrounded by landscaped gardens and a deer park. A fall from her pony at the age of fifteen probably damaged her spine but her famous ill-health may also have had psychological aspects – an intelligent young woman living with her ten siblings in the shadow of a dominant and secretive father must often have found life very trying.

She also longed for the formal, if rather brutal, education that was the norm for boys of her class. Hungry for intellectual stimulus, in her early twenties she became very fond of a blind classical scholar, Hugh Boyd, who lived with his wife and daughter in Malvern Wells in a house called Ruby Cottage. She regularly visited in order for him to help with her Greek and, in return, for her to read to him. Her diary covering this period shows how she tormented herself wondering when next she might see him, whether she meant more than other

HOPE-END
NEAR
LEDBURY.

Hope End in the early nineteenth century.

young women to him and how anxious she was about meeting new people or even about venturing from the security of her room or her home. Most unusually intellectual for an early nineteenth-century, young woman, and her mother having died in 1828, she agonised in 1831–1832 when threatened with the loss of her regular contact with Boyd in addition to the trauma of departure from Hope End. The collapse of her father's investments in sugar plantations in Jamaica finally put an end to the idyll of life at Hope End in 1832 and the family spent three years in Sidmouth before moving to London. The relationship with Boyd eventually became much less important to her and, after her secret 1846 marriage to Robert Browning, she lived in Italy, dying in Florence in 1861. Margaret Forster's very readable biography reveals that, despite often proclaimed support for the democratic ideals which gained considerable following in nineteenth-century Europe, the poet did not seem to practise these ideals in her own domestic affairs. She showed a disconcerting lack of feeling when her loyal and hard-working maids experienced family problems, her preoccupation with her own emotional and health needs not enabling her to show genuine sympathy for comparable difficulties in others. She did, however, have a genuine desire for the work of her husband to be recognised, and in her attitude to her servants she was naturally shaped by the conventions of her time.

She enjoyed considerable success in her lifetime and was suggested as a potential Poet Laureate, which would have been an astonishing achievement for a nineteenth-century woman. Her work fell from favour in the late nineteenth and early twentieth centuries, but with increased interest in the work of female writers, her reputation has recovered. Ledbury, however, always loyally valued its association with her, one of its landmark buildings being the clock tower of what became known as the Elizabeth Barrett Browning Institute, opened by the popular novelist Rider Haggard in 1896. In 1938 locally born Poet Laureate John Masefield opened the public library in the building. It is still there, but plans for its removal to another site are currently (2012) in hand.

In truth Elizabeth Barrett Browning seems to have spent little time in Ledbury, living in seclusion with her two sisters and eight brothers at the family home, with its eastern resonances and extensive grounds. Her poems 'The Lost Bower', 'Hector in the Garden' and 'The Deserted Garden', reflect her love of the Hope End grounds, and provide clear evidence of the permanent mark left on her by such a childhood home. In them she writes of the gardens, paths, orchards and surrounding woodland, and reveals her constant awareness of the Malvern Hills, which 'for mountains counted ... Keepers of Piers Plowman's visions through the sunshine and the snow.'[1] The Barretts' home was demolished in the 1870s, and the house that replaced it was destroyed by fire in 1910. Later, a high-class family-run restaurant and country hotel were established on the estate, also offering, under the National Gardens Scheme, the chance to wander in the beautiful grounds which inspired young Elizabeth Barrett.

---

1. From 'The Lost Bower,' published in 1844.

Mary Elizabeth Sumner (1828–1921)

Like Elizabeth Barrett, Mary Heywood, better known as Mary Sumner, came to Hope End at the age of three, when her rich parents, Mary and Thomas Heywood – he had been a banker – moved from Swinton, near Manchester and bought the Hope End estate from Elizabeth Barrett's father in 1832. The children were well educated and the family travelled abroad, so in no sense could Mary's childhood have been described as deprived.

She grew into a talented young woman who spoke three languages and was an accomplished musician at a time when musical evenings round a piano were a staple ingredient of family and social life. Young Mary was a cut above this, with a voice good enough for her singing teacher in Rome to recommend an operatic career. This never materialised because in July 1848, at the age of nineteen, she married, in Colwall Church, George Sumner, son of the Bishop of Winchester and related to the reformer William Wilberforce. It proved to be a happy marriage, lasting over sixty years and producing two daughters and a son. George Sumner, educated at Eton and Oxford, was a clergyman who for thirty-four years served as Rector of Old Alresford. He became Archdeacon of Winchester and then, in 1888, was appointed suffragan bishop of Guildford, which was then part of the Winchester diocese. He died in 1909 at the age of eighty-five and Mary died in 1921 aged ninety-three, having founded the Mothers' Union.

It was her establishment of the Mothers' Union that made her famous. She witnessed within her own family the concern of mothers to do the right thing by their husbands and children, and felt that her own experience of the power of Bible reading and of prayer might be helpful to others. The Union soon appealed to all classes because it recognised that young mothers often found it hard to cope with the responsibility of bringing up children and the stresses of family life; it also offered the opportunity for fellowship in the sharing of those anxieties.

From modest beginnings in the 1870s in Mary Sumner's own Old Alresford Rectory, when she was so shy that she was unable to speak to the assembled women, the movement became a nationwide, and eventually a world-wide, arm of the Anglican Church. She overcame her shyness to become a most effective and diligent speaker, chairing meetings all over the country until her eighties. Even in today's very different world, the Mothers' Union, which has its headquarters in Mary Sumner House, Westminster, is still a force to be reckoned with.

Mrs Henry Wood (1814–1887)

Ellen Price, later Mrs Henry Wood, was born close to Worcester Cathedral in 1814, and was the daughter of Elizabeth and Thomas Price: he was the rich and scholarly owner of a glove-making factory, a trade for which Worcester was famous. As a child she loved excursions to the little village of Malvern, but when she married in 1836 she went to live for about twenty years in France, returning to England in 1856 by which time her husband's business interests seem to have collapsed. She became famous as the writer of some forty books, which showed her interest in relationships, especially love and marriage and, more practically, earned her a goodly fortune. *East Lynne* is perhaps her most famous work, a huge success right from the start when it was serialised in the *New Monthly Magazine*. 'A Life's Secret' was serialised in *The Leisure Hour* in 1862 and when, five years later, she became the owner and editor of the magazine *Argosy,* she wrote many of its serialised stories herself, including the Johnny Ludlow stories which drew on her youthful recollections of Worcestershire, though she had lived in London since her return to England from France.

Her prodigious output and high earnings, at a time when few women were able to earn a decent living, are particularly remarkable in view of her indifferent health and problems with her spine. The growth and increasing sophistication of Malvern were not to her taste.[2] She died in February 1887 and was buried in Highgate cemetery.

Mary Brandling (1823–1873)

Mary Brandling has become something of a local celebrity through her

---

2.   William Lee, [article] *Malvern Gazette*, 24 June 1988, p.29.

THE LEISURE HOUR

A FAMILY JOURNAL OF INSTRUCTION AND RECREATION.

"BEHOLD IN THESE WHAT LEISURE HOURS DEMAND,—AMUSEMENT AND TRUE KNOWLEDGE HAND IN HAND."—*Cowper.*

SUNSHINE AFTER CLOUDS.

A LIFE'S SECRET.
CHAPTER XXI.—CONCLUSION.

"DID it never strike you that Austin Clay knew your secret?" inquired Dr. Bevary of Mr. Hunter, when he was left alone with him after Austin's departure in search of Florence.

"How should it?" returned Mr. Hunter.

"I do not know how," said the Doctor, "any more than I know how the impression that he did, fixed itself upon me. I have felt sure, this many a year past, that he was no stranger to the fact, though he probably knew nothing of the details."

No. 543.—MAY 24, 1862.

"When did *you* become acquainted with it?" rejoined Mr. Hunter, in a tone of sharp pain.

"I became acquainted with your share in it at the time Miss Gwinn discovered that Mr. Lewis was Mr. Hunter. James, why did you not confide the secret to me? It would have been much better."

"To you! Louisa's brother!"

"It would have been better, I say. It might not have lifted the sword that was always hanging over Louisa's head, or have eased it by one jot; but it might have eased you. A sorrow kept within a man's own bosom, doing its work in silence, will burn his life away: get

PRICE ONE PENNY.

This front cover of *The Leisure Hour* shows the prominence given to Mrs Henry Wood's serialised story 'A Life's Secret', which appeared in twenty-one instalments over the period 2 January–24 May 1862. The magazine carried few illustrations and the pictures on the front page of each weekly issue reflect the popularity of Wood's writing. Most other articles in the publication were factual, informative and of a somewhat 'improving' nature.

Welland Church painted by Mary Brandling in 1856.
Courtesy Malvern Library.

talent for drawing and painting. Her work forms a fascinating record of the places close to where she lived in the mid-nineteenth century.

Born in Exmouth to Mary and Charles Gifford, she was widowed in her early thirties and in 1856 married Lieutenant-Colonel John James Brandling, of the Royal Artillery, whose well-to-do family resided in Gosforth, Northumberland. This marriage soon produced three daughters, born in Canterbury, in Norwich and in Leeds so presumably her husband's army career took her to various homes throughout the country. He died in 1860 aged only thirty-eight, and the 1861 census shows her to have been a widow of thirty-seven living at Mousley House in Welland, which may have been on Assarts Common. She seems to have remained in this area for the rest of her life, dying in Worcestershire in May 1873. She left effects worth less than £800, probate being granted to the fourth Baron Lilford, a well-known ornithologist and the husband of her late husband's sister. Her real legacy was, however, her work.

Malvern Library has a good collection of her paintings, many acquired in the late twentieth century, which have been exhibited from time to time and are well worth seeing.

Florence Nightingale (1820–1910)

So much has been written about Florence Nightingale, especially in recent years to mark the anniversary of her death in 1910, that this is not the place to repeat it all. Her connection with Malvern lies in the numerous visits she made, starting in the 1840s, to take the water-cure. She found hydrotherapy very helpful in overcoming the desperate exhaustion and illness resulting from her ground-breaking work during and after the Crimean War of the mid-1850s.

Jenny Lind (1820–1887)

Jenny Lind, whose astonishingly pure soprano voice caused her to be nicknamed the Swedish Nightingale, spent her final years in Malvern, where she died in 1887 in her home, Wynd's Point, British Camp. Born in Stockholm in 1820 she started singing in public as a child and was appointed Court Singer to King Carl Johann by the age of twenty. Modest, shy and sometimes almost paralysed by stage-fright, she avoided the scandals frequently associated at that time with women who sang and acted in public: she travelled with a respectable female companion and stayed in the homes of well-to-do families with good connections. When she stayed with the Bishop of Norwich and his family they conversed in French because she found English much more difficult to learn than German, French and Italian: in her later

Eschewing make up and constantly having a chaperone, Jenny Lind maintained an air of simplicity and innocence for many years. Here she is shown in her youth.

years, after living in England for over thirty years she still spoke English with a strong accent.

She quickly became the darling of music lovers all over Europe, the peak of her fame coming in the 1840s and early 1850s, when a 'Jenny Lind Crush' became the term for the wild scenes that her

Jenny Lind on stage.

Wynd's Point where Jenny Lind died.

presence caused. At her first London performance in 1847 Queen Victoria was so delighted that she threw her own bouquet on the stage in tribute to a young woman – a year younger than herself – who could pack opera houses and whose picture on a chocolate box or souvenir could generate spectacular sales. The Swedish Nightingale's reaction to an unknown admirer's gift of a beaker full of ants' eggs, the favourite food of nightingales, is not clear – and the source does not reveal whether the eggs were real or, like the beaker, golden.[3]

In America from September 1850 until May 1852, she gave about one hundred and fifty concerts, said to have earned her well over £35,000. Her vast earning capacity was very advantageous to the numerous charities to which she made handsome donations: in 1849 she sang in Worcester in College Hall, some of the proceeds going to fund a chapel at Worcester Royal Infirmary. A particularly generous supporter of hospitals, she was uneasy at accepting the expensive gifts of jewellery – usually bracelets – that some grateful beneficiaries wished to bestow upon her by way of thanks.

---

3.   Joan Bulman, *Jenny Lind,* p.198.

Left: the memorial set up in 1894 in Poets' Corner, Westminster Abbey.
Right: Jenny Lind's grave-stone in Malvern cemetery.

She seems to have been emotionally insecure for years: she was twice engaged to be married but the engagements were amicably broken probably, it must be admitted, to the advantage of her public appeal as a demure and vulnerable performer. Numerous men, some married and some famous, seem to have been infatuated with her: Chopin was enchanted by her voice and Hans Christian Andersen seems to have been besotted with her. She worked very closely with Mendelssohn and was distraught at his early death in 1847. Unable to sing his songs for the next two years, by the time she was thirty she changed the nature of her performances: instead of opera, which required acting, she concentrated on religious oratorios.

In 1852 in Boston, Massachusetts, she married Otto Goldschmidt, a composer and her accompanist, some seven years her junior. He looked even younger and bore a resemblance to Prince Albert, Queen Victoria's husband. Some people compared not only the two women, Victoria and Lind, but also their two German husbands. The Goldschmidts settled in England in the late 1850s, by which time her voice, damaged by years of practice and performances, was beginning to deteriorate and her figure was developing the plumpness of a mature woman after the birth of two sons and a daughter, who later married Raymond Maude and came to live in Herefordshire. In her early sixties Jenny Lind became the first Professor of Singing at the newly established Royal College of Music in South Kensington[4] but visits to her daughter attracted her to Malvern. Two old cottages at Wynd's Point were converted into a home for herself and her husband, and her last public performance was in 1883 at the Spa Hall, close to the Wyche Cutting. It was a typical act of generosity: she sang, at the request of a Great Malvern Railway Station porter, at a concert in aid of the Railway Servants' Benevolent Fund.

She died of stomach cancer in 1887. After a funeral which caused Malvern to turn out in respectful droves with, among nearly a hundred floral tributes, a wreath from her old admirer the queen, she was buried in the cemetery in Wilton Road, where her husband was also laid to rest some twenty years later.

(Caroline) Alice Elgar (1848–1920)

The life of Sir Edward Elgar's wife has been eclipsed by the reputation of her husband whom she married in 1889 and to whom she devoted the remaining thirty-one years of her life. Her maternal grandfather was a clergyman and her great grandfather was Robert Raikes who did much to establish Sunday Schools. She was related to distinguished military men: her father, Major General Sir Henry Gee Roberts, and her uncle on her mother's side both served in India, where she was born. Famously, she therefore came from a higher social class than her husband, the penniless son of a piano tuner who ran a shop in Worcester. In class-ridden Victorian England their marriage caused consternation in her family. Differences in age – she was eight years older than Elgar – and in religion – she was Church of England and he a Catholic – complicated matters still further.

---

4.   Joan Bulman, *Jenny Lind,* p.314.

As a talented young woman who spoke several languages, she had literary aspirations and a keen interest in the work of the Gloucestershire antiquary, Revd W. S. Symonds, Rector of Pendock. Living in Redmarley, she started to have piano lessons with Elgar in the mid 1880s and was clearly a more apt and receptive pupil than many of those he reluctantly taught in order to earn a somewhat uncertain living. The lessons continued when she moved to Malvern: when they became engaged Elgar wrote *Salut d'Amour* as an engagement gift whilst she wrote him a poem which he set to music.

They were very poor in the early years of their marriage: one often recounted economy was her ruling out staves on plain paper to provide him with music paper as they could ill afford proper score paper. She was nearly forty-two – not young to be having her first baby – when she gave birth to their only child, Carice, in 1890. They lived in various homes in London and Malvern: the most well-known local ones are Forli in Alexandra Road, Malvern Link and Craeg Lea (an anagram of the names E, A and C Elgar) in Malvern Wells. For several years around the turn of the nineteenth century, when fame was beginning to come to Elgar, they also rented in the summer months a cottage at nearby Birchwood in Storridge.

Like Elizabeth Barrett Browning, Alice Elgar was a wife keen to support and protect a talented husband but, unlike her, failed to achieve fame in her own right despite early promise as a poet and novelist. Michael Kennedy quotes from her diary 'that the care of a genius is enough of a life work for any woman.' Recent research has led to rumblings that, despite valuing the security and honours of their later life, Alice became hurt and perhaps disillusioned at always playing second fiddle to a talented man with many admirers, a fondness for bicycling (often accompanied by lady friends) and something of an eye for a pretty woman.

Alice Elgar died of lung cancer in London in 1920 but her body was brought back for burial in the churchyard of St Wulstan's Roman Catholic Church in Malvern Wells, where her husband was later buried in 1934.

Marguerite Radclyffe Hall (1880–1943)

Marguerite Radclyffe Hall's large financial inheritance at the turn of the century, when she was twenty-one, scarcely compensated for a desperately unhappy childhood with parents who divorced each other and showed no affection for their only surviving child. She grew into a woman whose affected manner and love of flouting convention, brave though she may have thought it, did not readily endear her to others, though she might have condemned them as hidebound by respectability. Society's acceptance of lesbianism has been a hard journey for many women and Radclyffe Hall's attitude is unlikely to have helped them. Her political views were very right-wing and anti-semitic, while at a personal level she does not seem to have been a very kind partner, friend or employer. Believing herself to be a man trapped in a woman's body, she adopted the name John, dressed in an attention-seeking masculine fashion and considered her partner to be her wife. Clearly a deeply unhappy woman, without any evident sense of humour, she spent her life searching for an identity, her novels leaving the reader with a sense of the sadness, frustration and melancholy which seems to have permeated their author.

Numerous affairs preceded her first lasting love affair with a woman more than twenty years her senior – Mabel Batten, known as Ladye, with whom she lived in Malvern in the early years of the twentieth century. Having converted to Roman Catholicism in 1912 she may well have attended St Wulstan's Church in Malvern Wells, fairly close to her home. After Ladye's death in 1916 she took up spiritualism for a few years and developed her second major relationship. Her new partner, Una Troubridge, was still in her late twenties and the wife of a vice-admiral. The two women lived in various homes in different parts of the country but there were numerous long visits to France and Italy. Rich, self-assured and demanding, they were volatile in the treatment of staff who might be dismissed on a whim. From 1934 Radclyffe Hall tormented Una by having a passionate affair with a Russian nurse and, after several years of ill-health, died of bowel cancer in 1943. She is buried in Highgate cemetery. Long before modern legislation enabling civil partnerships and twenty-first-century ideas about same-sex marriages, Una thought of herself

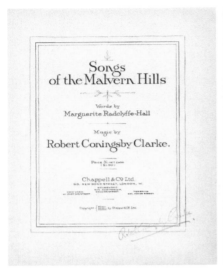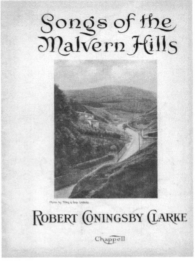

Radclyffe Hall's dedication in *Songs of the Malvern Hills* to
Mabel Batten, her deceased lover, and a flirtation with
spiritualism after the latter's death may reflect the
writer's regret about the way she had treated her.

as having had a long-lasting marriage with Radclyffe Hall, whom she
outlived by twenty years.

Before embarking in the 1920s on a career as a novelist, Radclyffe
Hall wrote poems and songs, several of which were published as
Songs of the Malvern Hills. Despite her dyslexia, recorded by her
biographer Diana Souhami, she wrote eight novels of which *The
Unlit Lamp,* published in 1924, is a well-written attempt to illustrate
the conflicting demands on an intelligent young woman, and today
would be considered a rather sad and tame commentary on the
very real difficulties faced by women who were, and are, pulled
in several directions by the diverse roles they wish or are required
to undertake. *The Well of Loneliness,* banned in 1928 on grounds
of obscenity, is, in truth, another quite tame effort, portraying
affection between two women. At the time of the obscenity trial
it was defended by the likes of Virginia Woolf and H. G. Wells.
Doubtless the good people of Malvern followed events with
particular interest: for those who managed to read it, the book's

opening words set it firmly 'Not very far from Upton-upon-Severn – between it, in fact, and the Malvern Hills.'

Dame Laurentia McLachlan of Stanbrook Abbey (1866–1953)

The Benedictine convent of Stanbrook Abbey, designed by Edward Welby Pugin in 1871, is very close to Malvern so perhaps it is excusable to include its long serving abbess, Dame Laurentia McLachlan, as a Malvern woman of note, especially since a friendship developed between her and George Bernard Shaw, a key figure in the pre-war Malvern Festivals.

In 2009 the nuns moved to their new abbey in North Yorkshire but Stanbrook was home to the successors of French refugee nuns who fled to England in the 1790s, after they were evicted from their home in France during the French Revolution. During their years at Stanbrook the nuns established a reputation for their music – Gregorian chant – and for high quality printing, especially of religious works. Given these facts, it is not surprising that they also had a reputation for remarkable women at the helm of their various activities.

One of these was Dame (the title is given to professed nuns) Laurentia McLachlan who served as abbess from 1931 until her death in 1953. Born in Lanarkshire in 1866 she was sixty-five and somewhat frail when she became abbess but she had long been recognised as a leading authority on the plainsong that was used in singing the daily services of the religious community, as well as a history scholar, especially in the field of the religious life. She also had a kindly understanding of human frailty and was a much loved leader with a sense of humour.

Her disciplined mind enabled her to hold her own in argument with men like the atheists Sydney Cockerell and Shaw. Between the three of them there developed a somewhat unlikely friendship. This was conducted in person and by letter, she being, as Shaw put it, an enclosed nun with an unenclosed mind.

A vital source of information on this remarkable woman is *In a Great Tradition,* a tribute by the Benedictines of Stanbrook led by her successor as abbess, Dame Felicitas Corrigan.

Dorothy Howell (1898–1982)

Few people now recognise the name of Dorothy Howell, a local pianist and composer who was once the focus of huge nationwide interest: in the 1920s she was a star attraction at major concerts including the Promenade Concerts established by Sir Henry Wood. Born into a musical Roman Catholic family and brought up in Birmingham, she displayed musical talent from an early age and, following convent education, studied at the Royal Academy of Music from the age of sixteen. She was to spend forty-six years of her long life teaching there as professor of harmony and counterpoint.

Much of her composition was inspired by the scenery around her: despite teaching in London, she spent a good deal of time in more rural surroundings and served during the Second World War in the Women's Land Army. In addition, her religious convictions led to the composition of church music and to her support for the Society of St Gregory, founded in 1929 and still very active in its efforts to keep liturgy and music alive in the church. In her later years, living in Malvern Wells, she was able to spend time with the nuns of Stanbrook Abbey, for whom she wrote several important pieces, and also to tend the grave of fellow Roman Catholic Edward Elgar and his wife. She died in her eighty-fourth year in Perrins House, Moorlands Road, Great Malvern and, like the Elgars, was buried in the graveyard at St Wulstan's, Malvern Wells.

Catherine Frances Severn Burrow (1871–1957)

Catherine Frances Severn Burrow was the daughter of a businessman, John Severn Burrow, and his wife. He founded the W. and J. Burrow mineral water company and also supported ventures such as the bringing of the railway to Malvern, the building of Holy Trinity Church and the establishment of Malvern College. He was one of Malvern's Town Commissioners in the middle of the nineteenth century, and his daughter inherited this interest in local government, becoming in 1919 the first woman member of Worcestershire County Council. She had a particular interest in education and gave the site for the West Malvern Open Air School. Serving as Chairman of the Malvern Education Committee for twenty years, she was

THE ABBEY GATEWAY BEFORE ALTERATION, 1860

Among the illustrations used by Miss Severn Burrow in *A Little City Set on a Hill* was this romantic 1860 drawing by Oldmeadow of the so-called Abbey Gateway before its north side was dramatically altered by the addition of a parapet and an extension on the right in 1891. In fact, Malvern Priory never reached the status of an abbey and the building shown here had living accommodation in it, so should more properly be called the Priory Gatehouse.

very keen to have a grammar school in Malvern, and supported the Malvern Technical School and School of Art: many believed that its building in Albert Road North was to become Malvern Grammar School. Although this did not happen, the building has for nearly ninety years been the hub of all kinds of technical, artistic and vocational study, still serving the local community as part of South Worcestershire College in a manner which would have pleased Miss Severn Burrow.

Her interests and energy were enormous and she had particular concern for people who were disadvantaged. Women were often in this category in the period during and after the First World War, so it is understandable that she was a pioneer and first president of the National Council of Women, as well as a promoter of the early Women's Institute movement. She was the founder in 1920 of a public utility society – Barnleigh Housing Association - which provided flats and bungalows for poorly paid single women at Barnard's Close, in Barnard's Green, and Pickersleigh Close in Malvern Link. Although its *raison d'etre* has in the ninety years of its existence been extended to include men and retired people, it is proof of her vision that, like her work for education, her efforts on housing have proved of long lasting benefit.

She also had talent as a painter who exhibited at the Royal Academy and was an architect and a pupil of Elgar, who taught her to play the violin. Her efforts as an historian are preserved in her delightful little book, *A Little City Set on a Hill*, which was published in the late 1940s when she was in her late seventies. She dedicated the book to her friend, Jean Corke Garrett, who lived near Miss Severn Burrow's home, Puck's Mead, Moorlands Road, close to Malvern Link Common. Mrs Corke Garrett herself wrote a little, a particular effort being *The White Witch of Welland,* a play intended for performance by local Women's Institutes. She based it on *The Shadow of the Raggedstone,* a novel which Charles Grindrod wrote in the nineteenth century to suggest that ill fortune will befall anyone over whom the shadow of Raggedstone hill falls.

Dame Laura Knight (1877–1970)

Laura Johnson came from a family poor in material possessions but led by an artistic and diligent mother who, aware of her daughter's promise, saw that she was trained at nearby Nottingham School of Art. There she met fellow artist Harold Knight whom she married when she was twenty-six. After some time in London and Holland, they moved to Newlyn to join the talented nest of artists keen on working outdoors in the very special light conditions of Cornwall. After the First World War they had working trips to America but were based in London, where Laura was able to work backstage depicting the dancers of the Diaghilev Company. Highlights of the interwar period were her 1927 election as an associate of the Royal Academy (only the second woman to have achieved the honour) and her 1929 appointment by George V as a Dame of the British Empire. By this time she had immersed herself in circus life, wandering around Bertram Mills' Circus in order to record the performers, both human and four-legged.

Her old friend, Sir Barry Jackson, started the Malvern Festivals in 1929 and the Knights started to attend the festivals regularly, hobnobbing with other big names in the art and literary world, such as George Bernard Shaw. She was the first woman Royal Academician, being elected in 1936 as a full member of the Royal Academy, an honour bestowed upon Harold a year later. By this time they were well acquainted with the Malvern area, spending a good deal of time in Colwall.

At the Nuremberg Trials of war criminals after the Second World War Laura Knight was appointed as an official war correspondent, her dramatic portrayal of the accused being fittingly exhibited at the Imperial War Museum. From Nuremberg she wrote of her experiences to Harold back in the Park Hotel in Colwall, where he was to die fifteen years later in 1961. She outlived her husband by nine years and died at home in London at the age of ninety-two.

The wide range of her subjects and techniques marks her out as a woman of exceptional ability and innovative ideas. Her remarkable achievements earned her many awards and her work can be seen in numerous galleries in London and abroad.

In 2008 Colwall Village Society erected a commemorative plaque in the Park Hotel, in the grounds of which she had owned a studio where much of her work was produced after the Second World War.

Catherine Moody (1920–2009)

Many people in Malvern treasure memories of this remarkable woman who died in 2009 at the age of eighty-nine. Her mother was a talented artist and her father, the artist Victor Hume Moody, was head of Malvern School of Art from 1935 in the building supported by Miss Severn Burrow and opened in 1928. Steeped in this artistic inheritance, young Catherine first studied under her father at Malvern, going on to the Royal College of Art and to Birmingham College of Art before teaching at the Manchester College of Art. She came back to Malvern, succeeding her father in 1962 as head of Malvern School of Art until retirement in 1980. Retirement, however, is hardly the right word for one so enthusiastic in so many fields throughout her long life.

Familiar with many talented and well-known artists, she was very talented herself, securing numerous prizes in a lifetime of

An early twentieth-century picture of St Ann's Well.

tireless drawing, painting and, especially, her work with pastels, sometimes combining them with other media. Her activities included encouragement of, and respect for, the work of others. A warm and generous hostess, she invited countless enthusiasts to her home, embellished with beautiful murals executed by its gifted owners. She left a permanent mark on Malvern Writers' Circle and the Malvern Art Club, as well as Malvern Architectural Society, which she founded. The unstinting time, energy and talent she gave to them all help to show the breadth and the depth of her interests and knowledge. Her passion to preserve Malvern's Victorian buildings led to her research which ensured that, when Great Malvern Railway Station was refurbished in the 1970s, the painted capitals on the pillars supporting the roofs over the platforms exactly matched the originals. Her 1953 book *The Silhouette of Malvern,* illustrated with numerous examples of her own artistic skills, epitomised her love of the town and its heritage. She also designed the gates erected at St Ann's Well to commemorate another talented woman, Joyce King, who edited the *Malvern Gazette* from 1945 to 1965. This period in the newspaper's history is regarded by many as unsurpassed in terms of quality of articles and coverage of news.

Even in the closing months of her long life Catherine Moody had plans for Malvern's future – not perhaps entirely feasible, but certainly the product of an innovative and dedicated lover of Malvern. Her funeral cortege, with wicker coffin seen through the glass of the hearse drawn by two beautiful horses on a chilly morning a week before Christmas, was a dignified and fitting end to the life of one who did so much for the town she loved.

The gates of the St Ann's Well were designed by Catherine Moody as a tribute to Joyce King, editor of the *Malvern Gazette* for twenty years.

CHARACTERS OF MALVERN

Malvern has been home to several very interesting women who are remembered with a variety of emotions including gratitude, amusement, pride and curiosity. They are certainly a mixed bag. There are, of course, all those women whose support of their husbands enabled the men to make their own mark as teachers, businessmen, doctors, scientists and leaders of social and political life in the town and its neighbourhood. But there are some women who made a mark in their own special way. We may all have our favourites; the following are mine.

Maria Ballard (1829–1915)

In 1854, at the age of twenty-five, Maria Bird of Yaxley in East Anglia decided, with some misgivings, to marry. Her bridegroom was bachelor Stephen Ballard, twice her age with a considerable reputation as a civil engineer and associate of the much more famous Thomas Brassey. For some months after the marriage they lived in Holland, where Ballard worked on engineering contracts, but settled down to spend the rest of their married life in Colwall, where he had bought the extensive Winnings estate on which he built a modern farmhouse, complete with central heating and a porch where passing vagrants learnt to stop for a bowl of soup and a few kind words. The amount of work for Maria was considerable – her husband reckoned that 5,800 bowls of soup were given away in a year.

Both were full of concern for the unfortunate: she driven by strong religious convictions and he with less interest in organised religion but determined to do the decent thing by his fellow men. Like Lady Henry Somerset, she was a passionate supporter of the temperance movement and, with her husband's financial and practical support, secured the building of the Workman's Hall at Colwall Stone as a place to which men could resort without being tempted to drink alcohol. She and her daughters also achieved the building of two nonconformist chapels in Colwall. In nineteenth-century Colwall, where there was no resident doctor, nurse or chemist, Mrs Ballard was also the instinctive first port of

Maria Ballard.
Courtesy Freda Ballard.

call for those in need of medical help: she kept a cupboard full of medicines and bandages, and her daughter recalled how she could stitch up a gash in an injured hand or provide herbal remedies for a wide variety of infirmities.[1]

The marriage was, despite the cautionary advice of those who had urged her not to marry a man so much older than herself, one which produced four sons and four daughters, one of whom wrote of what an excellent combination they made – father young for his years and with a twinkling sense of humour and mother old for her years and totally lacking one.

Florence Bravo (1845–1878)

Florence Bravo was Malvern's nineteenth-century *femme fatale*. Born

---

1.   Pamela Hurle, *Stephen Ballard*, p.86.

in Australia in 1845 she came to England in 1857 with her wealthy parents to live at Buscot Park – a large and imposing house set in beautiful Oxfordshire parkland and now in the hands of the National Trust. The family also had homes in Knightsbridge, London and in Brighton. A few days after her nineteenth birthday Florence married rich twenty-one-year-old Alexander Ricardo, who unfortunately became an alcoholic in his mid-twenties. Desperate, she came to Malvern in 1870 and soon became a patient – and very close friend – of Dr Gully, who for the last twenty-eight years had been making a fortune from the Malvern water-cure and had become a respected pillar of society and local government in the fast developing town. Old enough to be her grand-father, he fell for her youthfulness and beauty, and she for his charisma and position.

News that her husband's condition was getting worse led young Mrs Ricardo to contemplate a legal separation but, having left Malvern for Buscot and then London, she was given the news in the spring of 1871 that her husband had died in Germany in the company of another woman. Mrs Ricardo had become a very rich widow at the age of twenty-five.

Her relationship with Dr Gully deepened: many people believe that they were lovers and that he performed an abortion on her in 1873. Like so many suggestions in the sorry story, this has never been proven, but seems quite possible. He had in 1871 retired from his practice in Malvern, going to live near her in Streatham, London, and they spent time abroad on holidays together in Italy and Germany.

In 1874 Mrs Ricardo moved to a large house with extensive grounds in Balham, interestingly with the same name as Dr Gully's Malvern home – the Priory. In December 1875, having ended her relationship with Dr Gully some time before, she married her second husband – Charles Bravo, a young barrister attracted by both her beauty and her wealth. He died in mysterious circumstances four and a half months later: antimony was found in his body and, to this day, no-one knows how it got there, causing him to take three days to die very painfully.

Two inquests attracted huge and, for Mrs Bravo and her family, humiliating interest, which did permanent damage to their reputation and health. Dr Gully's association with the young widow meant that the manner of her husband's death also tarnished his reputation. It transpired that his groom had signed the poisons book when purchasing from the pharmacist in Church Street, Malvern a quantity of tartar emetic, which contains antimony, for veterinary use on Gully's horse. Was this the same poison that killed Bravo? Gully was not personally involved in the events of that terrible night when Bravo drank the poison, but many questions, unanswerable at the time, made life difficult and embarrassing for everyone concerned in any way at all, however peripherally. Bravo, like Ricardo, was a heavy drinker. How did the poison get into his glass? Who administered it? Was it suicide? Was it accidental in the sense that this particular poison was used in small quantities as a form of aversion therapy to overcome alcoholism? Was it murder? Modern forensic methods would have been able to clear up the matter even though Bravo's vomit had been washed away before the arrival of the medical and police experts. But scandal, innuendo and gossip could not be put to rest in the 1870s.

Nevertheless, when Gully died in Balham, aged seventy-five, in 1883, Malvern's local press put black edging round his obituary as it mourned the passing of the man who had so much increased the town's prosperity. He outlived Florence Bravo, who died of alcohol poisoning in September 1878 aged just thirty-three.

Polly Cartland (1877–1976)

Polly Cartland, like her famous daughter Barbara, lived to a great age, having been born in 1877 and dying in 1976. In 1931 she bought Littlewood House, Barnard's Green, formerly the home, then called Peckham Grove, of Lady Lyttelton. A seemingly fearless driver who learned to drive before a driving test was deemed a basic safety requirement, in her later years Polly Cartland was still driving her little car around Malvern, apparently believing in the principle that at a junction it was all right to drive on, so long as one did it slowly. And then to park at right angles to the kerb if the more general practice of parking parallel to it was not possible.

In fact, there was much more – and much to admire – in this lady who became one of Malvern's characters. According to her daughter,[2] who clearly adored her and would brook no criticism of her, she was beautiful, kind and fun-loving, but with a social conscience and a strong Christian faith which led to her conversion to Roman Catholicism in the late 1930s. She certainly needed some such inner resources since her life was one of considerable sadness: her husband Bertram was killed in May 1918 during the closing horrors of the First World War and, exactly twenty-two years later, her two beloved sons, Ronald and Antony, died within a day of each other in the 1940 Allied retreat from Dunkirk. As with so many such tragic family losses, many months passed before she was told the sad news. Through those months she had cherished the belief that at least one had survived. Her only surviving child was Barbara, who had attended schools in Malvern and Worcester.

The family mixed with the rich and famous, as Barbara was keen to point out in her biography of her mother. Although they never knew grinding poverty, Polly had a struggle to keep up the life-style to which she had been born – reduced to having only one maid and having to do her own cooking. In the early struggles after her husband's death she opened an upmarket London dress shop to bring in some money and keep up at least some appearance of a comfortable life-style. As she famously pronounced, 'Poor I may be – common I am not.' She later threw herself into supporting her son Ronald in his successful bid to become an MP and carried out all kinds of good works before, during and after the Second World War.

The Community of the Holy Name

In 1879 a community of nuns bought land and two houses in Ranelagh Road, Malvern Link with the intention of continuing in Malvern the kind of worship, mission and social work they had undertaken in the poverty-stricken Vauxhall area of London since 1865. When they arrived in Malvern Link their newly purchased property was in a rural position with superb views towards the Malvern Hills; opposite was the home of the priest whom they regarded as Father

---

2. Barbara Cartland, *Polly, My Wonderful Mother.*

The chapel designed by Sir Ninian Comper for the Community of the Holy Name
Courtesy Peter Smith.

Founder, the high church Revd George William Herbert, one of whose daughters was to marry the son of the vicar of Great Malvern, Canon Pelly. Much of the nuns' early work was with 'fallen women', some of whom came from London to Malvern with them. Under a succession of devoted and practical Mothers Superior the community's property was extended to include accommodation for the sisters and those whom they helped. Sir Ninian Comper designed a simple but beautiful chapel in the early 1890s. Missionary work at home and abroad was an important feature of their lives but all sisters had to come back to the mother house at Malvern Link at least once a year. Their work for unmarried mothers became much less significant with the spread of contraception and the acceptance of single mothers, and by the 1970s they were seeking to emulate the convent at Stanbrook and develop skills such as book-binding. In 1990 they moved to Derby to continue their worship and outreach – a word which has recently come into popular jargon to describe the efforts of churches and charities to provide visits, services or support to a wide circle of people who might otherwise fall through the net of social or religious activities. Never having been an enclosed order, as they went about their work they had a presence in the town which was a part of Malvern life now quite forgotten. Their once beautiful buildings have already deteriorated, and in particular the fate of Comper's chapel is still uncertain.

ALSO REMEMBERED

Miss Caley
A member of the chocolate manufacturing family, Miss Caley was another well-known Malvern character. Renowned for her carefulness with money – but generous in her quaint way - she drove her horse and trap even at night through the streets of Malvern, sometimes to deliver, for example, logs to those she thought deserving. It was said that she died from asphyxiation when the piping to her gas-fire started to leak because the horse, lying on bedding in the sitting-room, dislodged the fitting.

Betty Snowball
Betty Snowball was a renowned female cricketer who played for England from 1934 to 1949. After retiring from competitive cricket she came to live in Colwall when she was appointed to teach mathematics and cricket at the Elms School. She died in 1988 at the age of eighty, and in 2011 Colwall Village Society erected, at the village cricket club's pavilion, a plaque in her memory.

Sue Thetford
For nearly forty years Sue Thetford was a Malvern Hills Conservator, serving as its Chairman from 1982–1985. She stood out in three ways: above all, her passion for, and knowledge of, the hills meant that she never missed anything that was happening on them, and knew exactly what powers were vested in the Conservators. Secondly, she was a woman who commanded respect in what had been largely a men's sphere of interest; thirdly she was instantly recognisable as she drove an old open-top red Alvis around Malvern in all weathers. She died at the age of seventy-six in 2010.

REFLECTIONS

This short examination of the achievements of women of different social classes in the last two hundred years helps to put on record the contribution that they have made to life in Malvern and further afield. For most of the period under discussion women were regarded, whatever their social standing, as inferior to men in intellectual as well as physical strength. They did not enjoy voting rights equal to those of men until 1928 and had to wait much longer for equal pay: even in professions demonstrably demanding comparable talents, such as teaching, fully equal pay was achieved barely fifty years ago. This is partly explained by the distinction perceived in the educational needs of boys and girls – itself a commentary on how women were regarded. Such distinction slowly became blurred not only as the result of calamities such as world war, but also as the result of pioneering headmistresses like those mentioned in this book. It was a very lengthy process of adjustment, and some might say that there is still some way to go.

It took generations for society to grasp the significance of economic independence for women: without an independent income women depended on men. Fathers, husbands and brothers were the usual benevolent, or otherwise, controllers of their lives. Many of the women mentioned in the foregoing pages were unusual in having control over their own lives, a phenomenon resulting not only from their innate talents or drive but also from being unmarried or widowed and thus able to be themselves rather than appendages of the person who controlled the purse-strings.

An illustration of how women were treated – and a hint of things to come – is afforded by a little scene on the Malvern Hills in June 1899. When the wife of the chairman of Malvern Urban District Council unveiled the toposcope on the Worcestershire Beacon as a belated mark of Queen Victoria's Diamond Jubilee she was presented with a printed silk copy of its phosphor-bronze plate as a memento. Her husband, Dr Dixey, felt it a privilege to be allowed to return thanks on her behalf but noted that probably it would not much longer be necessary for gentlemen to answer for them on occasions such as this.

It has been a long and eventful journey.

BIBLIOGRAPHY

Baird, Alice, *I Was There* (Littlebury, 1956).

Bannister, Christine, *Apphia, Lady Lyttelton* (Aspect Design, 2011).

Bede, Cuthbert, 'Malvern Donkeys', *Leisure Hour* (1862).

Benedictines of Stanbrook, *In a Great Tradition* (John Murray, 1956).

Berridge, Elizabeth (ed), *The Barretts at Hope End* [an early diary of Elizabeth Barrett Browning] (John Murray, 1974).

Black, Ros, *A Talent for Humanity: The Life and Work of Lady Henry Somerset* (Antony Rowe, 2010)

Bridges, Yseult, *How Charles Bravo Died* (Reprint Society, 1957).

Bulman, Joan, *Jenny Lind, A Biography* (James Barrie, 1956).

Burrow, C. F. Severn, *A Little City Set on a Hill* (1949).

Cartland, Barbara, *Polly, My Wonderful Mother* (Arrow Books, 1971).

Chambers, John, *A General History of Malvern* (1817).

Chester-Lamb, Kate, *Eventful Days* (St James School, 1997).

Community of the Holy Name, *History of the Community of the Holy Name 1885–1950*.

Dixey, Mary, Duseline Stewart and Sheila Barker, *Lawnside the History of a Malvern School* (Lawnside Old Girls' Association, 1996).

Dray, Glenys, 'Mary Brandling', *Malvern Wells Newsletter* (2011).

Fitzpatrick, Kathleen, *Lady Henry Somerset* (Cape, 1923).

Forster, Margaret, *Elizabeth Barrett Browning* (Chatto and Windus, 1988).

Fray, Stanley J., 'The Artistic Community in Late Victorian Malvern,' MA dissertation (2008).

Graham, James, Duke of Montrose, *My Ditty Box* (Jonathan Cape, 1952).

Grindrod, Charles, *Malvern Guide* (*c.* 1860).

Hall, Marguerite Radclyffe, [Radclyffe-Hall] *Adam's Breed* (1926).

— *The Forge* (1924).

— *The Master of the House* (1932).

— *Songs of the Malvern Hills* (1916).

— *The Unlit Lamp* (1924).

— *The Well of Loneliness* (1928).

Holland, Henry Scott and W. S. Rockstro, *Jenny Lind the Artist* (Murray, 1893).

Hurle, Pamela, *Bygone Malvern* (Phillimore, 1989).

— *Malvern Girls' College, A Centenary History* (Phillimore, 1993).

— *The Malverns* (Phillimore, 1992).

— *Stephen Ballard, One of Nature's Gentlemen* (Aspect Design, 2010).

Hurle, Pamela and John Winsor, *Portrait of Malvern* (Phillimore, 1985).

Jenkins, Elizabeth, *Dr Gully* (Michael Joseph, 1972).

Kennedy, Michael, *Portrait of Elgar* (Oxford, 1987).

Keynes, Randal, *Darwin, His Daughter and Human Evolution* (Riverhead, 2002).

Knight, Laura, *The Magic of a Line* (Kimber, 1965).

Lee, William [article on Mrs Henry Wood] *Malvern Gazette,* 24 June 1988.

Malvern Advertiser, Obituary of Lady Emily Foley, 6 January 1900.

Maude, Mrs Raymond, The Life of Jenny Lind (Cassell, 1926).

Mike, Celia *Oxford Dictionary of National Biography,* entry on Dorothy Gertrude Howell (1898–1982), (OUP, 2004) http://www.oxforddnb.com

Mitchell, Sally, *Oxford Dictionary of National Biography,* entry on Ellen Wood (Mrs Henry Wood 1814–1887), (OUP, 2004) http://www.oxforddnb.com

Moody, Catherine, *Silhouette of Malvern* (Priory Press, 1953).

Moore, Jerrold Northrop, *Edward Elgar, A Creative Life* (Oxford, 1984).

Niessen, Olwen, *Aristocracy, Temperance and Social Reform: The Life of Lady Henry Somerset* (Tauris Academic Studies, 2007).

Pinches, Sylvia, *Ledbury, a Market Town* (Phillimore, 2009).

Porter, Mrs Horace, *Mary Sumner, Her Life and Work* (The Mothers' Union, 1927).

Postle, David, *A Glimpse of Old Ledbury* (Amber Graphics, 1988).

Ruddick, James, *Death at the Priory* (Atlantic Books, 2001).

Souhami, Diana, *The Trials of Radclyffe Hall* (Weidenfeld and Nicolson, 1998).

Southall, Mary, *A Description of Malvern* (printed for the author by G. Nicholson, 1822).

Taylor, Bernard and Kate Clarke, *Murder at the Priory* (Grafton, 1988).

Thomas, R. N. W. *Oxford Dictionary of National Biography,* entry on William Harcourt, Third Earl Harcourt (1743–1830) (OUP, 2004) http://www.oxforddnb.com

Turberville, T. C., *Worcestershire in the Nineteenth Century* (Longman, 1852).

Where to Buy in Malvern (c. 1891).

Williams, Dorothy E., *The Lygons of Madresfield Court* (Logaston Press, 2001).

Worcester Evening News and Times, Obituary of Miss C. F. Severn Burrow, 1 August 1957.